Computer Programming Bible

A Step by Step Guide On
How To Master From The
Basics to Advanced of
Python, C, C++, C#, HTML
Coding Raspberry Pi3

C.P.A. Inc.

professional before attempting any techniques outlined in this book.

By reading this document, the reader agrees that under no circumstances is the author responsible for any losses, direct or indirect, which are incurred as a result of the use of information contained within this document, including, but not limited to, — errors, omissions, or inaccuracies.

Table of Contents

Introduction

The decision to start programming is considered a life-changer for a lot of people today. Many programmers consider themselves a higher species, given the knowledge that they have amassed over the years. Programming makes the world go round, as some would say. After all, a lot of what we do today involves computers in one way or the other.

From the moment you decide to join the world of programming, you must realize that your life will never be the same again. You are not just going to work with computers, you will understand them in a way you never imagined. The role of a computer is to make work easier, solve problems faster, more efficiently and so on. If you learn how this works, you are in a good position to do so much with your computer.

Programming is about giving the computer instructions to follow. Computers are machines. They act on the set of instructions we feed into them. Without this information, the computer is just like any other machine. Save for the latest modern technology that includes AI, machines that are built to think on their own and act independently upon studying some variables, computers basically take what you feed them and deliver output.

In terms of feeding the computer data and expecting output, this is where programming comes in handy. There are many things you can do with a computer. To communicate effectively, you must input the right instructions. Through programming, you learn different languages that enable you to communicate with computers at different levels.

Each program is essentially lines of code that are executed depending on the input you key into the device or application you use. Some programs are very simple, others are quite complex. However, the foundation of all programs is code.

When you start programming, there are many languages that you might need to learn. Each language is unique in its own way, even though you will realize there are a lot of similarities among them. C programming, for example, is widely considered the basic starting point for most programing languages. What this means for you is that learning and mastering C programming will go a long way in helping you succeed in your endeavors as a programmer.

Building from C, you will come across other programming languages like C++, C#, Python and so on. At the moment, there are more languages than you can imagine. Given the unique nature or projects and programs that are used in different environments, at times it is advisable to have unique languages specifically built for a given program. In as much as this is the case, many of the languages still borrow a lot from the predominant languages like C and Python.

This programming guide introduces you to the major languages that you should learn, which will form the basis of your understanding of programming going forward. More often, it is the basics that beginners fail to grasp that affect their ability to advance to higher learning in programming. This guide is written with relevant and useful examples to help you learn step by step.

The journey that lies ahead is an incredible one. There are many projects that you will build based upon the information you learn from this book. The best foundation will help you build your career in programming without fear. More importantly, remember that like math, it takes a lot of practice and persistence to be good at programming.

Programming is essentially about finding problems and solving them in the most efficient way. Go out there and enjoy yourself while at it.

Chapter 1:

Why Should You Learn

Computer Programming?

The idea of computer programming is something that we have to contend with today. Think about it, computers are everywhere. We use them in virtually every aspect of our lives. From the time you wake up in the morning, all through your day until the moment you go to sleep, you interact with computers in different forms. Wouldn't it be amazing if you were able to learn as much as possible about these devices that almost control your life?

Computer programming is about instructing computers on the next step. Basically, that is what computers do, they take instructions and deliver results. Computer programming enables you to learn about computers from the most basic instructions to more complex ones where computers make decisions independently, based on advanced machine learning algorithms.

Computers help us in solution finding. They make work easier, reduce the workload and improve efficiency. The best case for this is in the industrial market where more industries are increasingly being computerized to improve efficiency and reduce waste in production processes.

Some people fear that one day in the future, computers might take over and replace our jobs, but this is not true. In as much as computers improve efficiency, an element of human control and monitoring is still necessary to ensure that they perform as they should. This is where knowledge of computer programming comes in handy.

When you understand how programs run, you can easily monitor and amend processes to ensure things run smoothly. For those who are afraid of job loss, one of the best things about computer programming is that it has created so many opportunities, many of which are yet to be filled. A simple search online will reveal so many jobs associated with computer programming. The vast majority of these jobs are things that you can perform at home without having to go to an office. This means that while a sector of the workforce might be afraid of the future of computing, an enlightened majority can see the amazing prospects that are available and take advantage of the opportunities.

In computer programming, the end result is always to build something. It could be a complex program or a simple script. This explains why computer programming is more than just learning about computers, it is an elaborate blend of science and art. Computer programming requires analytical skills and technical know-how that can elevate you to major success in the near future. For creatives, programming helps you leverage your skills and talent in a world that is crazy about new technology.

As you venture into programming, one of the burning questions you will probably ask a lot of people who have been in the industry for a while is which programming language is the most suitable to learn. Think about programming like your curriculum in school. There's a blend of different subjects, from math, science, social studies, finance, music and the arts.

Of course, you might not need all the subjects considering your preferred career path. You might not even be good at them. However, all the subjects are connected in one way or the other. Even if they do not appeal to you, learning them makes you a better person. It allows you to be enlightened enough to interact with people who take a keen interest in the subjects that you are not so skilled in.

Say you graduate from college and specialized in math. However, in your course, you also had some classes in psychology and the social sciences, but you were not so good at them. You can engage other individuals who specialized in those subjects later on. When you meet them at a gathering, you can have a hearty conversation, learn more about one another and appreciate their perspective. This is what happens in programming too.

There are many programming languages out there that you might come across. To be fair, you do not necessarily have to learn all of them. However, there are some basics that you should learn. Even if you do not focus a lot of your attention on them, the knowledge will come in handy from time to time as you encounter different projects.

One of the guiding principles when choosing the right programming language to learn is to think about your core objectives and goals in your career path. Do you plan to focus on websites and related development or are you planning to delve deeper into building apps?

The interesting thing about computer programming is that many of the languages you will come across share so much in common. Their syntaxes allow you to transfer knowledge of one language to another, boosting your grasp of the techniques involved.

Whether you want to learn a language or not, at some point you might find the knowledge useful. Programming is an ongoing activity. This is also a defining convention in programming. The world of IT is constantly evolving. Some of the things that were life-changing developments in 2015 are no longer the rage in 2019. That is how fast things change in the world of IT.

For a programmer, one of the best ways to stay ahead of these changes is to master as many languages as you can. Keep engaging in projects that challenge your thought process and encourage you to think beyond the ordinary. This will help you set yourself on a path to versatility, and it will be difficult to miss an opening that you cannot fill.

Back-end and Front-end Programming

There are two aspects involved in computer programming that might guide you on your choice of programming language or your career path. Front-end and back-end programming involve access to the programs you build. Front-end programming is about writing code which has results that appeal to the users. It is usually about the look and feel of the program. You are basically building projects for the clients.

Back-end programming, on the other hand, is about ensuring the project you build works smoothly. Back-end programming is the engine of the project. Users might have access to and enjoy the beautiful graphics on the project, but behind the scenes you do the dirty work. You interact with the code behind the project, which is not visible to the users.

These two aspects of programming are important in different ways. As a front-end programmer, for example, your work is to appease users. You are constantly thinking of ways to attract them, keep them on the website or program longer. The longer they stay on the project, the more you devise other ways to get the users to act on something.

Basics Every Programmer Should Know

What does it take to become a good programmer? Computer programming is a never-ending learning process. Whether you are a beginner, intermediate or expert programmer, you learn each day. Some people would tell you the idea of a great programmer is relative, because it is almost impossible to learn and know everything in programming. How good you are might also depend on unique factors like the kind of project you are working on or the language you specialize in.

Whichever the case, there are a few things that you should master in order to consider yourself a good programmer. These are features and factors that apply to different scenarios all the time and will definitely apply in your programming life too. They are basics that all programmers must know.

Learn a language

This might sound obvious, but you'd be surprised at the number of people who call themselves programmers, yet they don't understand any programming language.

There are many languages that you can learn in programming, some of which you might never use in the foreseeable future. However, what you should do is master at least one language.

For example, Java is one of the simplest and easiest languages you can learn. You don't need prior programming knowledge. You can start with this. Or, perhaps you prefer Python because of the easily understandable language and library support. The choice is yours, but at least make sure you are good at something.

Networking

You don't necessarily need to have a CCNA certification for this. There are simple networking tasks you should not have to rely on someone to perform for you. The world is getting increasingly networked and interconnected on a regular basis, and we are getting to a point where all the devices, products and appliances we use are linked together in some network.

Besides, most of the programs that you write have to communicate through a server, so understanding the basics of networking will be a useful step. If you can learn some networking at beginner level, you will be better off because you can advance both your networking and programming careers at the same pace.

Data manipulation

You will use a lot of data in programming. From data collection to analysis to reconciliation, data is everywhere. You might write code to perform a task, but the code is simply the skeleton of the program. The program is brought alive when you introduce the right kinds of data into it.

One tool you must learn to use is Microsoft Excel. Excel can do so much more than serve as a spreadsheet. Learn some formulas and how to use them. Learn how to filter, sort, search and use the depths of Excel beyond basic clipboard functions. This will be useful in programming.

IDE

You cannot be a programmer without learning to work with an IDE. The right environment allows you to work with your preferred language without struggling. If you are programming in C#, C++ or C, Visual Studio is the ultimate choice. Python programmers will prefer Jupyter Notebook. You can use any IDE that you are comfortable with.

Text editors

Text editors are very basic, but they are powerful. Each computer comes with a native editor installed. However, if you need advanced capabilities, you can install third-party editors like Notepad++ or Sublime. Each editor has unique features, shortcuts and productivity tips that make your work easier when writing code.

Reasons for Learning Programming

At this point in time, you probably realize you will need to learn some computer programming at some point in the near future. The good thing is that developers are trying to make programming as easy as possible. For parents, it is wise to introduce children to programming at an early age, so they get the prerequisite skills to enable them to compete favorably in the job market in the near future.

Here are some of the reasons why learning programming is a brilliant idea for you:

- Efficiency and productivity

There isn't a stronger case for learning computer programming than the need to improve productivity and efficiency. We already admit that computers have become a normal part of our lives. Since we cannot wish them away, why not use them to make our lives more productive in every sphere?

One of the challenges that many people struggle with today is the inability to find enough time for themselves. We are too busy doing so many things that we can barely rest. This takes a toll on the body and eventually erodes our performance down the line.

Through computer programming, you learn how computers work and how to write simple programs that will help you spend less time doing the things that normally consume your time. In the long run, you end up with more time to rest, interact with your loved ones or try your hand at something new.

Learning how to write code can help you change your life infinitely. By understanding how computer programs work, you can write simple programs to automate important aspects of your life, making your life much easier.

- Collaborative approach to management

Teamwork is important to fulfil most of the tasks we are required to at work. In teamwork, there's a lot of back and forth and information exchange that takes place to enable the projects or programs run smoothly.

Everyone in your team has a different understanding of concepts and instructions you are working around. While others grasp new information so fast, some team members are relatively slower. Working independently would slow down the entire team.

Through programming, however, you learn how to collaborate with different teams. From time to time you will need to explain some concepts to your team members so that they realize what's at stake. Other than that, you might also have to break down some ideas in such a way that everyone can understand them better.

When you understand the people you work with, it is easier to write programs that address their needs. You can also offer tutorials to help those who struggle to catch up with everyone else. In the long run, this collaborative approach will be fruitful for the entire team.

- **In-depth knowledge of systems**

You use a lot of programs and systems each day. Have you ever stopped for a moment and thought about how that program or machine does what it does? How is it that you simply insert your debit card at an ATM machine, key in your PIN or password and get money from your account?

Assume time travel were possible. Imagine living in 1920 and traveling to the year 2019. The technology would shock the daylights out of you. Worse still, the indifference with which you'd see people going about their lives would mesmerize you.

In-depth knowledge of systems is, however, not about time travel. It is about understanding how your inputs are processed to deliver the output you desire. You learn about how the system interacts with your data to deliver the output you see. What if you change the nature of your input? Would the output be the same?

There are good job prospects for you in this niche. Companies are always looking for program testers before they release a new program. If you understand how the program works, you can identify bugs, recommend fixes and so much more.

- **Dynamic approach to solution finding**

Computers are built to make our work easier. They solve problems faster than we would. For example, a teacher would have to key in all the subject scores for a class of 50 students manually, get a calculator and compute their totals. From there, they would calculate other mathematical computations like the average and median. All this is for one subject. Imagine the frustration when they have more than five subjects.

However, with Microsoft Excel all the teacher needs to do is key in the correct scores from the students' papers and the program will compute all the necessary calculations in an instant. Excel is one of the simplest programs you can use to solve many problems faster.

Beyond Excel, you can also learn to write programs to help you solve some of the issues you deal with at home or at work. We struggle with high energy costs, especially because we need to keep our homes habitable, even when we are not around.

Through programming, developers have created systems that allow you to monitor your home even when you are away. You can control the heat, light and humidity all from the click of a button.

- Modern age creativity

Programming is a unique industry. It allows you to combine talent and technical know-how. This is one of the reasons why we have a lot of creative designers in different fields today. Say you are a professional photographer. Without programming, your work would only revolve around taking photos, editing them and sharing them online. With programming, you can take things a notch higher. You can create an ecommerce store to sell your photos.

One of the best things about programming is that you must be on toes all the time. Things are always changing, especially when you look at your target audience in terms of their tastes and preferences. You can learn a lot of useful programming skills to leverage your creativity and set yourself above the rest.

- Appreciating effort and value recognition

How many times have you received a quote for some services and wondered why the provider is asking for too much money? Value addition and value recognition go hand in hand.

Today the world is angled towards a culture where people appreciate value. If you are not adding value to someone's life, or even to the company, you are deemed an unnecessary surplus.

When you learn to write code, you can begin to understand why programmers charge an arm and a leg for their work. Building an interactive website, for instance, is not an easy task. It takes a lot of time, resources and skill. If you have ever tried it, you understand what it takes and why a developer would send you the kind of quote they did.

Appreciating effort also helps you become a better manager. You recognize the amount of work that goes into building a project from scratch and you understand why you should pay what the developer asks for. Besides, it can also help you avoid the risk of paying too much for something mundane.

- Perform mundane tasks

In 2019, you will still be surprised to find someone who does not know how to open a simple blogging account. These might seem like very simple and mundane things, but they are a big deal to some people. Children as young as six years old are building amazing interactive websites already. These are things that were the preserve of experts and companies in the past.

Indeed, building a website is a big deal. Depending on the kind of website you want, it takes so much more than knowledge of CSS and HTML to get the ultimate site. One of the best things about this is that with your knowledge of computer programming, you can create websites and build apps, in the process saving on money that you would have spent on production and recurrent maintenance.

Possible Challenges You Will Face in Computer Programming

Starting a career or interest in computer programming is a bold move. There is so much that is in store for you if you continue down this path. We have seen some of the reasons why a career in computer programming is a very good move for you. However, it is not always a smooth ride. There will be bumps along the way and you should be prepared for them.

Here are some of the things that you should be aware of going forward:

- **Insane competition**

It is no secret that computer programming is one of the most competitive fields out there. Since a lot of people are waking up to the fact that programming is the prerequisite to being an efficient employee some years down the line, it makes sense that more people are learning programming. Prepare to face competition from experts, some who are experienced in other fields and are adding computer programming to their portfolio.

Computer programming is not just a preserve for programmers, you will meet journalists, athletes, musicians, painters and other artists who are very good at programming, you'll struggle to understand why they don't take it up as a full-time job. You will actually come across very good programmers who have never been to a class in university but can make the world stop when they sit down at their keyboards.

- **Communication challenges**

The fact that you spend a lot of time on your computer or brainstorming with other programmers on the way forward will affect your communication skills with non-programmers. One thing you will do a lot in programming is translate normal language to computer language and back.

At some point, you might find yourself more drawn towards computer languages because of the thrill of the unknown. After all, you probably know all you need to know about your native language. Computer languages, on the other hand, are a whole new world that's ready for exploration.

Many expert programmers spend more time on computers than interacting with people because human interaction is full of mistakes and flaws. While debugging a computer language delivers immediate results, it is impossible to debug a human being. Therefore, they end up withdrawing and focusing on something with a result that is instantly achievable programming.

- Persistent fatigue

You will be constantly bombarded with new technologies, conventions and skills that you must learn to stay ahead of the pack. Learning new technology is not easy. Learning too many new programs at the same time is even harder. While you might succeed and grasp the information over time, your risk of fatigue will be higher.

- Health concerns

Here's one thing that many successful programmers never tell you: your health will suffer along the way. The better you are at programming, the more sought after you are. At this point, even the kind of projects that you handle will have scaled up. You will not be working on simple scripts or writing basic code but working with some major projects that demand a lot of your time, specificity, and attention to detail.

Repetitive strain injury, internet addiction, and the usual risks of a sedentary lifestyle are some of the health concerns you might have to deal with. From time to time you will feel strain in your eyes from staring at your screen for too long. You will also be spending some sleepless nights trying to debug some code or rushing to meet an impossible deadline. With some careful planning, you can find a way around these risks though.

- Upgrades

Prepare for upgrades. Some of the upgrades will annoy you, but you have to run them anyway. Assuming you are using different programming languages at the same time, given the nature of your job, keeping up with upgrades can be very frustrating.

Other than the upgrades, you also need to learn more about new libraries all the time. Libraries are added into the programming languages to make work easier for programmers. Understanding new libraries, APIs and languages will be a regular thing for you. Many times, you will come across something new and rush to search engines to find out more about it.

Generally, you will invest a lot of energy, effort and time in staying abreast with the latest developments in the industry, because you never know what the next client will demand for their project. Staying at the top will not be easy, but it is worth your struggle.

Think about the students who study programming in college. By the time they graduate, most of the stuff they learn is either outdated or obsolete. They have to start learning new languages and improve on the skills they learned in class to be ready for the demanding job market.

- Uncertainty

If there is one thing that you must be aware of about computer programming is that the future is not always easy to predict. Given the dynamic nature of advances in the tech world, it is not easy to tell when a new convention might make your specialty obsolete.

To be fair, there are so many programming languages in use at the moment that learning all of them at the same time might be very difficult. At the same time, you have to be adept at most of them if you are to thrive in a highly competitive environment. Bearing this in mind, it is almost impossible for you to tell what the future holds, other than the fact that change is always imminent.

You don't have to go so far to identify some popular technology that people were excited about that is no longer as glamorous as it used to be. At times the difference between the in thing and obsoletion could be as brief as one year or a few months.

- **The occasional boredom**

If there is one thing that programmers loathe, it is the people who see them as the ultimate fixers. You are a programmer, not a hardware technician. Many times, people will come to you with problems that you cannot handle and feel disappointed when you turn them away.

There are also those who assume you have the answer to every computer problem they come across. After all, they see you working on your keyboard all the time, not mentioning those who assume you are a hacker, or should probably stop working and start your own Facebook or whatever in-thing that everyone will be excited about at that moment.

These risks aside, programming is a very good career path. The benefits outweigh the risks. There is a myriad of opportunities available for you in this industry, some that you are not even aware of yet.

The role of programming in the future is unimaginable. What we know for sure is that learning about programming right now sets you on the right path. Your determination will help you become one of the best in your field.

Chapter 2:

Programming in HTML

Webpages use HTML as the standard markup language. This is one of the first languages you should master in your programming career. HTML is the foundation of programming, especially if you plan on focusing on websites. It is also one of the easiest languages to learn.

HTML means Hypertext Markup Language. Basically, what this language does is describe how a website is built. Your browser then picks up on these descriptions to display content accordingly.

HTML elements are enclosed in tags, with every tag labeling specific content. Tags include things like *"paragraph"* and *"heading."* The browser will not show the HTML tags, but they are used in the background to help you access the content in a pleasing manner.

This is what an HTML document looks like:

```
<!DOCTYPE html>

<html>
<head>
<title>Title of your Page</title>
</head>
```

```
<body>

<h1>Write Heading Here</h1>
<p>Paragraph begins here</p>

</body>
</html>
```

The description above has some elements that you notice in each HTML webpage you access. What do they mean?

- *<!DOCTYPE html>* - This is an identification that you are accessing an HTML document.

- *<html>* - represents the root of the webpage

- *<head>* - this is where all meta information about this document is contained

- *<title>* - this is where the title of your document goes

- *<body>* - this is where the content you are accessing goes. It is made up of paragraphs, media content and any other information you need

- *<h1>* - this is an element that indicates the type of heading used in the document.

There are many other heading types available

- *<p>* - this element denotes where each paragraph begins

You will also notice that HTML tags are usually written in pairs, such as <> and </>. These are opening and closing tags. HTML is like accounting. All accounts must always balance. If you perform a transaction on one account, a similar transaction must affect another account in the same amount. In HTML, if you use an opening tag, you must use a closing tag at the end of your action.

We mentioned earlier that HTML informs your browser how to display the content you are accessing. An opening tag *<h1>* shows the browser where the heading begins and tag *</h1>* where the heading ends.

Therefore, whenever you see an opening tag, there has to be a similar closing tag with a forward slash. The declaration tag *<!DOCTYPE>*, however, should only be used once at the beginning of your HTML document before you write any other code because it helps the browser identify the type of document. It does not use a closing tag.

There have been different versions of HTML over the years, with each release improving on the former and making work easier for programmers. Currently, HTML5 is the version used.

Editing HTML Documents

There are several professional editors that have been created for HTML. They have unique features that reduce the amount of work you have to do, especially by filling in some of the tags you need automatically. However, the best way to learn HTML is to learn the basics, then later on advance to the text editors.

A simple webpage can be created using the native text editor in your computer. For Windows users, Notepad is all you need, for Mac it is TextEdit.

Navigate to your text editor, open a new document and enter the basic HTML code we shared above.

Save the document as an HTML page, so that each time you open it, it displays on a web browser. To save the document as an HTML page, use the *Save as* feature and name the file i*ndex.html* or *index.htm*.

You can now open the file on your browser. One of the best things about working with HTML is that you can review progress as you proceed. Write a few sentences in the body of the document between the paragraph tags, save the document and refresh the browser page. The results should be instant, unless you messed up something.

HTML links are identified using the *<a>* tag. A link points to some website. The attribute *href* denotes the website in question.

In HTML, attributes give us more information about the element represented. For example, the element *<a>* shows you a link is present.

<a href=https://www.google.com Click on this></a> shows you the website you will be redirected to when you click.

You will also come across image tags in HTML. These are identified by *<img>*. Some of the attributes used to describe image tags include:

- Width

- Height

- Alternative text (alt)

- Source file (src)

An HTML line describing an image will look like this:

<img src="google.png" alt="google.com" width="100" height="158">

Buttons help in making navigation easier for users. They are represented by the *<button>* *</button>* tags.

You might need to create a list in HTML. You can use an unordered list, also referred to as the bullet list, with tags *<ul></ul>*, or you can use an ordered list, also known as a numbered list, with tags *<ol></ol>*, then you include the *<li></li>* tags for each item on your list. You will list your information within these tags.

Here's an example:

```
<ul>
  <li>BMW</li>
  <li>Mazda</li>
  <li>Toyota</li>
</ul>

<ol>
  <li>BMW</li>
  <li>Mazda</li>
  <li>Toyota</li>
</ol>
```

An HTML element is everything that is enclosed from the opening tag to the closing tag. There are unique elements that do not have closing tags. These are referred to as empty elements. One of these is a line break, which is indicated with *
*. You can also choose to close an empty element in the opening tag instead and write *
*.

As you study HTML documents, you will notice some elements can include many other elements within. This is referred to as nesting. For example, an HTML document contains a lot of HTML elements nested within.

There are some conventions that apply when using HTML which might not apply in other document types. For example, some closing empty elements are not mandatory in HTML, but you might have problems rendering the document on XML while HTML is not case-sensitive, it is advisable to strictly use lower case and get used to it, because this is the standard for other types of documents like XHTML.

HTML Attributes

We mentioned earlier that attributes give us more information about specific elements. You specify attributes within the opening element tag. An attribute is always displayed in a name=value pair.

Here are some examples of attributes used in HTML:

- href

This attribute defines a link within the <*a*> tag as follows:

<a   href="https://www.google.com">This   is Google</a>

- width and height

This attribute defines the dimensions of the image:

```
<img        src="img_google.png"        width="400"
height="500">
```

- src

This attribute defines the source of the image in the
<img> tag as follows:

```
<img src="img_google.png">
```

- alt

This attribute shows the browser what text to show in
case the images cannot be shown, or if the image no
longer exists.

```
<img src="img_google.png" alt="Google logo">
```

- lang

This attribute helps the browser determine the native
language used in the document. It is useful for
accessibility and can help in translating the document.
The attribute is included inside the *<html>* tag.

In the example below, *en* informs the browser the
document is in English, while *UK* identifies the dialect.

```
<html lang="en-UK">
```

- style

This attribute helps to the different styles used in an element. It includes things like the font size and font color.

`<p style="color:green">`The grass is green.`</p>`

Once again, remember to write your attributes in lower case, even though HTML does not demand you do.

While the browser can display some content properly when you don't use quotation marks around values, in some cases this might not work. Therefore, it is advisable that you always use quotes around attribute values.

If you are quoting an attribute that naturally has double quotes, you can use single quotes instead.

HTML uses six heading designations, from *<h1>* to *<h6>*. The headings are arranged in order of their importance.

Proper use of headings will help search engines index content on your website accordingly. Many users today glance at web pages by looking at the headings. Therefore, make sure you use the right headings around important titles.

HTML assigns a default size for every heading. You can change this using the *font-size* property in CSS as follows:

`<h1 style="font-size:65px;">`Heading 1`</h1>`

Once you feed data into the HTML document, it is impossible to tell what the display will look like. The results depend on the way the screen you use displays. Even if you add more spaces and lines into the code, the browser automatically deletes them. You can use the line break element *
* to indicate where the line ends.

So, how do you write music lyrics or poems? Do you have to write *
* at the end of each line? Not necessarily. In this case, you can use the *<pre>* element for preformatted texts. All text within this element maintain their line breaks and spaces.

Here's an example:

<pre>

How do I live without you?

How do I breathe without you?

You are everything I have.

Come back to me.

</pre>

HTML Styles

The style attribute helps you determine what style is used in the document. Style is enclosed in the syntax below:

<tagname style="property:value">

The property and values are CSS items.

Therefore, the background color for your webpage will be identified as follows:

<body style="background-color:black;">

You can also choose a specific color for your text for different sections of the content as shown:

<h1 style="color:green;">This statement is green</h1>

The paragraph continues

In the HTML document, you can also specify the font and font sizes to use:

<h1 style="font-family:Georgia;">The heading goes here</h1>

The paragraph goes here

<h1 style="font-size:240%;">The heading goes here</h1>

```
<p    style="font-size:150%;">The    paragraph    goes
here</p>
```

To align and display text accordingly, indicate the preferred style as shown:

```
<h1    style="text-align:center;">The    heading    is
centered</h1>
```

```
<p    style="text-align:center;">The    paragraph    is
centered</p>
```

Take note that all the attributes used in styling your HTML document are CSS properties.

Formatting Texts

There are many ways of formatting texts to highlight specific parts of the content. The following are some of the formatting elements you can use:

- *<small>* Small text

- *<sup>* Superscript

- *<sub>* Subscript

- <b> Bold

- *<ins>* Inserted text

- *<del>* Deleted text

- *<strong>* Important text

- *<em>* Emphasized text

- *<i>* Italic text

- *<mark>* Marked text

The elements above define the actions applied to a specific subset of texts within the webpage. These are just a few examples. There are more tags that you will come across as you learn HTML.

Comments

When writing HTML code, you might come across a situation where you need to add some comments into the source code. You need comment tags for this (/). Comment tags do not have a closing tag.

Coders use comment tags for reminders, especially when debugging their code. When you are going through the hundreds or thousands of lines of code you have written, the comment tag can help you make notes on the errors so you can review them later on.

Comment tags look like this in HTML:

<!- - Your comment goes here - ->

Colors in HTML

In HTML, colors can be identified in the following ways:

- Regular color name

- HEX values

- RGB values

- RGBA values

- HSL values

- HSLA values

Regular color names

This is the normal dictionary name assigned to colors. HTML supports more than a hundred color names, and can be assigned to different parts of your code as follows:

<hi style="color:Gray;"> This is My Page</h1>

HEX Values

This is a hexadecimal value form used to define colors. Colors are defined as #rrggbb. It also follows the red, green and blue convention, assigning values between 0 and 255. 0 is the lowest value, while 255 is defined as ff.

Defining color red in this method is #ff0000. All the values are set to zero, while red is set to the highest value. Blue is #0000ff.

Black in this convention is #000000, white is #ffffff and shades of gray in between white and black are balanced as #f0f0f0, #676767, #2c2c2c.

RGB Values

This system considers the colors red, green and blue (RGB) to assign values to colors. The three colors are the foundation of each color. Each color is a derivation of RGB at an intensity between 0-255.

Color red, therefore, is written as rgb (255, 0, 0). This is because red is the predominant value, and the other two are valued at 0.

In this convention, white is rgb (255, 255, 255) while black is rgb (0, 0, 0). Different forms of gray are derived by balancing all the shades between white and black, for example rgb (50, 50, 50), rgb (90, 90, 90) or rgb (175, 175, 175).

RGBA Values

This convention expresses colors as RGB but includes an alpha (A) channel to represent the opacity of the underlying color. Therefore, rgba represents (red, green, blue, alpha).

The alpha value represents opacity between fully transparent (0.0) and completely opaque (1.0).

The following are different shades of red under this convention:

- rgba (255, 98, 70, 1)

- rgba (255, 98, 70, 0.5)

- rgba (255, 98, 70, 0)

HSL Values

This value system considers color hues, saturation and lightness (HSL) when assigning colors.

Hue refers to a specific degree assigned to different colors on the color wheel. In a range from 0-360 degrees, the colors are apportioned as follows:

- 0 – red

- 120 – green

- 240 – blue

Saturation refers to how intense a color is, and it is assigned as a percentage, ranging from 0-100%:

- 0% - the underlying color is not visible anymore.

- 50% - this is a grayscale form of the color, though the underlying color is still visible

- 100% - this is the purest form of the color, without a shade of gray

Lightness is also assigned as a percentage as follows:

- 0% - black

- 50% - neither black nor white

- 100% - white

In this mode, colors are assigned as follows:

- Blue – hsl (240, 100%, 50%)

- Red – hsl (0, 100%, 50%)

HSLA Values

This convention considers the HSL color convention, plus an alpha value to denote the opacity of the underlying color. Therefore, the convention is represented as hsla (hue, saturation, lightness, alpha). The color red in this convention can be expressed in the following shades:

- hsla (9, 100%, 65%, 1)

- hsla (9, 100%, 65%, 0.5)

- hsla (9, 100%, 65%, 0)

Cascading Style Sheets (CSS)

The role of CSS in your HTML code is to define how the elements will be shown in any media form, whether it's on the screen or printed on a piece of paper. CSS is useful because it helps you organize a lot of pages at the same time.

There are three methods of embedding CSS into your HTML code:

- External – through external CSS files

- Internal – in the <head> section by inserting a <style> element

- Inline – through a style attribute in the HTML elements

While the easiest method is to use external CSS files, learning how to apply an inline CSS style is important as it helps you understand the context of the code. Inline CSS is applied as an HTML element attribute as follows:

<hi style="color:green;">This line is green</h1>

An internal CSS describes the style used in the entire HTML page. It is enclosed in the *<head>* of the HTML page as a *<style>* attribute as shown:

```
<!DOCTYPE html>
<html>
<head>
<style>
body {background-color: blue;}
h1   {color: powderblue;}
```

```
p    {color: black;}
</style>
</head>
<body>

<h1>The heading goes here</h1>
<p>The paragraph starts here.</p>

</body>
</html>
```

External CSS sheets describe the style that is applied to several HTML pages on your website. This is useful when building a website with several pages. Since the style applies to all the pages, making changes to the CSS file applies to each page simultaneously.

External CSS files are added as a link in the *<head>* of the HTML page as shown below:

```
<!DOCTYPE html>
<html>
<head>
  <link rel="stylesheet" href="styles.css">
</head>
<body>

<h1>The heading goes here</h1>
<p>The paragraph starts here.</p>

</body>
</html>
```

You create the external CSS sheet in any text editor. However, this document should not have any HTML code. Once the document is ready, save it with a *.css* extension so you can link to it. In the example above, in the *<head>* tag we linked to a *styles.css* sheet.

This external CSS sheet should look like this:

```
body {
  background-color: blue;
}
h1 {
                                    color: green;

}
p {
  color: black;
}
```

A close examination of the CSS code reveals more information like the color of the text (color), font size (font-size) and the type of font used (font-family) as shown below:

```
<!DOCTYPE html>
<html>
<head>
<style>
h1 {
  color: powderblue;
  font-family: georgia;
  font-size: 250%;
}
p {
```

```
  color: green;
  font-family: georgia;
  font-size: 150%;
}
</style>
</head>
<body>

<h1>The heading goes here </h1>
<p>The paragraph goes here.</p>

</body>
</html>
```

Using Links in HTML

All HTML links are hyperlinks. They allow you to move from one document to another online. Hyperlinks are identified through the *<a>* tag as follows:

```
        <a
href="https://www.google.com">Search on
Google</a>
```

All links have the following default color behavior unless you change them through the CSS sheets:

- Active links – red and underlined

- Visited links – purple and underlined

- Unvisited links – blue and underlined

It is also possible to change the color behavior of the links by editing your CSS sheet as follows:

```
<style>
a:link {
  color: orange;
  background-color: transparent;
  text-decoration: none;
}

a:visited {
  color: red;
  background-color: transparent;
  text-decoration: none;
}

a:hover {
  color: green;
  background-color: transparent;
  text-decoration: underline;
}

a:active {
  color: blue;
  background-color: transparent;
  text-decoration: underline;
}
</style>
```

If your webpage is very long, you can use bookmarks to help users ease navigation. You can create chapters and add links to them, making it easier for your audience. When they click on the link, it navigates to the specific location. An example is shown below:

```
<h2 id="C3">Chapter 3 </h2>

<a href="#C3">Jump to Chapter 3</a>
```

Possible Challenges When Programming in HTML

HTML is one of the basic structuring languages that you can use online. However, it has its unique challenges that might pose a challenge for beginner programmers. Some of the challenges are also experienced by expert programmers, so you should not feel terrible if you struggle. The good thing is that there are lots of support networks available where you can get all the help you need.

The obvious problem that arises when using HTML is that you need a browser to parse it properly. While you can read and interpret HTML code on a text editor or any other available outlet, the best option is always to use a browser. One of the challenges with this is that some of the browsers, like Chrome are very heavy on resource use. However, there are lighter browsers available, so this should not be as big a problem. After all, HTML was basically written to be read on browsers.

Security is a very big concern in HTML. There are lots of reasons for this. One of the programming concerns here is interpretation. Each author can interpret the code in the way they understand it best. The risk here is that your interpretation might not be the same as someone else's interpretation, which means that even when you do your best work ever, someone might still struggle to find sense in it. Interpretation also increases the risk of errors. By making the wrong interpretation, you can easily change the code and end up with terrible output on your screen.

Over the years, many of the languages used in programming have advanced in leaps and bounds, save for HTML. The technical advancement and progress have been hindered by a lot of reasons. This sluggish pace of development means that HTML has remained a slowly evolving language over time, as other languages keep improving. The good news is that there are improvements, especially in the advent of HTML5. There is still a lot to be done to raise the profile of HTML to the level that other languages have reached.

While interpretation is dependent on the programmer, one of the other inherent interpretation challenges you will experience when using HTML is the language. By default, American English is the preferred language in HTML. This is a problem for users who are not native American English speakers. There are ways to get around this, but the additional work makes it difficult especially for learners who cannot access the additional resources to get by.

HTML is not a functional language. It simply tells your browser what to do and how to display content you need. Hence, it is a declarative language. The problem with a declarative language like this is that beyond building a website, there is not much you can do with HTML. People frown upon HTML and it is considered the most basic of languages you can spend time on.

Some experts even find HTML a waste of time and talent, as they would rather focus on writing code in other languages that can be used to build amazing projects and make a significant impact in the world around them.

Another challenge you will experience with HTML is the struggle to update it. In fact, for the most part HTML updates are manual. In case you do not maintain your schedule, you can end up running an outdated version of HTML, which leaves your code and projects open to exploitation.

The manual update process is also not as simple as you would expect. It involves some script writing, which is too much work for some programmers, who would rather work with something else that is ready to go.

It is possible to add unique tags in HTML. This is something that many vendors have considered over the years. For example, Microsoft has done this in the past, and while the result is good, not all browsers can support custom tags. Therefore, it might not be feasible for everyone.

Chapter 3:

C Programming

C is one of the most flexible and popular general-purpose programming languages. C is used in structured programming and has been adopted by many applications over the years. C is the foundation of a lot of operating systems in use today, including Windows, and was also used in creating programs like Git and Oracle.

C is widely considered the foundation of programming, making it one of the prerequisites for anyone who wants to venture into programming for the long-term.

The following are some of the major instances where C programming is used today:

- Internet of Things applications

- Producing compilers

- Developing operating systems

- Database development like MySQL

- Creating browser extension and browsers

- Building desktop applications

- Building system applications

- Embedded systems

Being the foundation of most programming languages, understanding C programming will go a long way in helping you learn other languages faster. Most of the operators, data types and control statements in C are used in other languages too.

In C programming, programs are broken down into different modules. In so doing, you can write each module independent of the others and collectively all the modules form a C program. This concept makes your work easier during debugging, as well as for testing and maintenance purposes.

The efficiency of C programming comes down to the fact that it has effective built-in functions, unique data types and 32 keywords. Besides this, C is a programming language that can be extended through its library. Within this library, you are free to add functions and features you need to make your programs simpler and easier to use, especially when working on complex programs.

Perhaps one of the best reasons why, as a programmer, you should consider learning C is that it is a portable language. What this means is that most of the programs you write in C will easily run on other machines. This comes in handy, especially when you need to test or run some code on a different computer.

C programming is a compiler language. The role of a compiler is to convert a program into a model that machines can read. A program written in C goes through three stages: writing the source code, compiling the source code and finally linking the program to object files.

There are several compilers that you can use to execute programs written in C, such as Turbo C and Clang Compiler. To write or execute a program written in C on any machine, you must have the right environment installed, preferably an IDE. IDE is recommended because you get a debugger, editor and compiler bundled together.

Writing Your First Program

The following is a simple *Hello World* program written in C:

```
#include<stdio.h>          //Pre-processor directive

void main()                //main function

{

printf("Hello World"); //to output the string on a display
```

```
return ();                          //terminating function

}
```

Let's try to understand what the code means:

- ## Preprocessor directive

The preprocessor directive in C is *#include*.

#include<stdio.h> refers to the library where the *printf* function is present. This function is used to generate output. You have to indicate the necessary file *(header-.h)* before you use the *printf* function.

In C programming, you can easily create functions, cluster them in *.h* files and use them in the program you write.

The preprocessor directive is used to include files in a program as follows:

    #include <file-name>.h

The *file name* refers to the file containing the functions you are adding to the program. Remember that it is mandatory to write the pre-processor directives at the beginning of your program.

- ## Main function

The main function is present in any program written in C. It can be presented in several forms including the following:

- main ()

- main (void)

- int main ()

- int main (void)

- void main ()

- void main (void)

Why are some of the parentheses empty and others filled? An empty one is a sign that the function does not have any parameter, value or argument assigned to it. Alternatively, you can also use *void* to mean the same thing.

- Source code

Once you declare the main function in your program, you must also declare the opening and closing parentheses. In C, the beginning and end of a program is indicated by curly brackets { }.

The curly brackets must be placed right after the main function. All the code you write must be confined within the curly brackets.

The function *printf* passes the Hello World text, thence generating the output.

The end of the statement is indicated by the semicolon (;). This is another rule you must remember when coding in C.

Writing Comments in C

A comment explains or describes the source code. You might understand your code, but someone else might not. Therefore, comments help other developers understand your code better. Because comments can explain your logic, they will also help you when debugging.

You can have any of two types of comments in your code as shown below.

Single-line comments, start with a double slash (//) to comment on single lines:

// C program demo

// Single Line comment

#include <stdio.h>

int main(void)

{

    // An example of a single line comment

```
        printf("Hello World");

        return 0;  // return zero

}
```

Multi-line comments begin with slash asterisk (/*) and end in asterisk slash (*/). These comments can be written anywhere in the code, even on multiple lines:

```
/* This is an example of a multi-line comment

Comment 1

Comment 2

.....

Comment n

*/
```

Comments generally help to enhance readability and understanding of your code. It is wise to write code that is understandable by both humans and computers. Besides, the compiler will ignore all comments in your code, so they do not affect the code at all.

Character Sets

Character sets are instructions that, when executed properly, deliver the desired output. Character sets in C are made up of the following:

- Letters – lower-case and upper-case A-Z

- Numbers – all digits between 0 and 9

- White spaces – new line, blank space, horizontal tab and carriage return

- Special characters such as comma, period, tilde, underscore, apostrophe, colon, question mark, subtraction, caret, addition, ampersand, dollar sign, hash sigh and percentage sign

Tokens

Tokens refer to the smallest units in any C program. They are further classified into keywords, strings, operators, constants, identifiers and special characters.

All words written in C are either identifiers or keywords. Keywords in C have fixed meanings which cannot change. There are only 32 keywords in C, and they are all written in lower-case. They are as follow.

- while

- static

- if

- do

- volatile

- sizeof

- goto

- default

- void

- signed

- for

- continue

- auto

- double

- struct

- int

- switch

- long

- else

- break

- unsigned

- union

- return

- float

- short

- extern

- const

- char

- typedef

- register

- case

- enum

Unlike keywords, identifiers are not fixed. They are user-defined names you give elements when writing a program. The following rules apply when using identifiers in your code:

- The identifier name must mean something

- They must start with an underscore or an alphabet

- Identifiers must only be formed using underscore, numbers and letters

- You cannot use keywords as identifiers

- You cannot use a whitespace character in an identifier

Variables

Variables are identifiers that hold some value in the code. When executing the program, variables can change, and you can also update the values assigned to the variables, unlike constants. Variables are built from digits, characters and underscores.

You can use one variable in different parts of your program. When using variables, remember that they must have a reasonable name, an indication of its purpose. The variable *age* can be used to store the ages of different people in your code.

Before you use the variable, you must declare it. The following rules apply when using variables in your code:

- Variables must never have a keyword

- Variables must never have a whitespace

- Variables must never start with a numeral

- Variables must only contain underscore, digits or characters

- C programming is not case-sensitive.

The following is an example of declaring an integer variable *my-variable* assigned the value 75:

> int my_variable;
>
> my_variable = 75;

The example above can also be declared in a single statement as follows:

> int my_variable =75;

Data Types

There are specific data types that are allowed in C which you can use when writing different applications. The data types are as follows:

- User-defined

- Derived

- Primitive

When writing code in C, the following are the main data types you will be using:

- void

- char – character data

- int – integer data

- float point

- double

Integer data types

Each machine has a unique range of integer values used in data types. Generally, the range is between -32768 and 32767. Integer values consume 2 bytes. They are further broken down into long int, int and short int. Each of these types has a unique range.

The long int is used for long integer values, int for average values and short int for small values.

When writing a program in C, you must place int before an identifier before using the data type, as shown below:

int age;

In the example above, *age* is the variable and you can use it to hold different integer values corresponding with the description you need.

Floating data type

Floating point data types represent numbers that contain both decimal points and fractions. Integer data types cannot hold decimal points, hence the need for floating point data types.

Floats generally contain no more than 6 values. If this is not enough, we can introduce other data types that can accommodate the large values, like data type double and long double, which are used for holding data up to 14 bits and 80 bits.

An example:

float division;

double BankBalance;

Character data type

This data type can only handle one-character value.

An example:

char letter;

Void data type

Void data types are used to define C functions and they do not return any value.

An example:

void displayData()

The following is an example that shows the different data types discussed above:

```
int main() {

int x, y;

float salary = 12.31;

char letter = 'K';

x = 25;

y = 35;

int z = x+y;

printf("%d \n", z);

printf("%f \n", salary);

printf("%c \n", letter);

return 0;

}
```

Output:

60

12.310000

K

Constants

Unlike variables, constants are fixed all through the program. There are different types of constants as shown below:

- **Integer constant**

These are hexadecimal (0-9, A-F), decimal (0-9) or octal (0-7) integers.

Octal integers must always start with 0, for example, 019, 076 and 057.

Hexadecimal integers must start with 0X, for example, 0X4 and 0Xcbd.

Hexadecimal and octal integers are hardly used in C programming.

- **Character constant**

These constants include a single character in a single quote ("). In some cases, they have ASCII values assigned to them. Examples include 'B' and '8'.

- **String constant**

A string constant refers to a chain of characters inside a double quote (""). Examples include "Howdy" and "Writing."

- **Real constant**

Real constants contain fraction or decimal values, hence also referred to as floating point constants, for example 214.14, 302.00.

Conditional Statements

Programs written in C are sequential in execution. This means that for one thing to happen, something else must happen first. By introducing a condition in your statements, the execution will depend on the results of the conditions. This is what is referred to as decision making. The statements behind the decisions are known as control statements.

Conditional statements in C are made possible based on the following constructs:

- **If**
- **If-else**

If

If statements change the flow of the program upon execution. They must have conditions, which the program evaluates before executing the statement. The basic syntax of an *if* statement is written as:

if (condition)

instruction;

The result of this condition is either *true* or *false*. True results are non-zero values, while false results are zero values. Here is an example:

```c
#include<stdio.h>

int main()

{

        int num2=3;

        int num3=5;

        if(num2<num3)                          //test-condition

        {

                printf("num2 is smaller than num3");

        }

        return 0;

}
```

Output

Relational Operators

There are six relational operators used in C which are used to test conditions and make decisions, thereby answering the *if* statements as true or false. These operators are:

- *!=*   not equal to

- ==   equal to

- >=   greater than or equal to

- >   greater than

- <=   less than or equal to

- <   less than

One of the most common mistakes many programmers make is to use *(=)* to mean equal to instead of *(==)*.

Here's another example:

int x = 52;

x =x+ 2;

if (x == 54) {

printf("You succeed!");}

Output:

You succeed

It is also important to highlight that any condition that results in a non-zero value is deemed true in C. as shown below:

int present =1;

if (present)

printf("Someone is in the house \n");

Output:

Someone is in the house

If-Else

This statement answers the same questions as the if statement, with some extensions. The general syntax of an if-else statement is shown below:

if (test-expression)

{

True block of statements

}

Else

{

    False block of statements

}

Statements;

What happens in such a statement is that the true block of statements is only executed if the value is true. On the other hand, if the value is not true, the false block of statements is executed. Let's look at the example below:

```c
#include<stdio.h>

int main()

{
        int num=22;

        if(num<15)

        {

                printf("The value is less than 15");

        }

        else
```

```
    {

        printf("The value is greater than 15");

    }

    return 0;

}
```

Output

The value is greater than 15

If-else statements can also be represented with a conditional expression *(?:)*. This happens in a situation where you can only use one statement to evaluate the *if* and *else*. Here's an example:

```
#include <stdio.h>

int main() {

  int y;

  int x = 20;

  y = (x >= 60) ?  60 : x;/* This is equivalent to:  if (x >= 50)   y = 50; else    y = x; */

  printf("y =%d ",y);

  return 0;}
```

Output:

$$y = Z$$

Nested if-else statements

These statements are used when you need to insert an *if-else* statement inside another, especially when you need to make several decisions as shown below:

```c
#include<stdio.h>

int main()
{
        int num=10;

        if(num<100)

        {

                if(num==10)

                {

                        printf("The             value
is:%d\n",num);

                }

                else

                {
```

```c
            printf("The value is greater than
10");

        }

    }

    else

    {

        printf("The value is greater than 100");

    }

    return 0;

}
```

Output:

The value is :10

In the example above, your program asks whether the number is greater or less than 100 and prints the result.

Since there are several indentations in this program, you must be very careful so that the program is easily readable.

Possible Challenges When Programming in C

While C is basically the foundation of most of the programming languages that we use today, it is not free of fault. There are some challenges that you will encounter as you get used to writing code in C. Most of these are glaring challenges that you realize out of familiarity with some of the other languages you have used before.

One of the biggest challenges many people experience when programming in C is that there is no security guarantee for your code. At a time when the world is on high alert about privacy and security, you have to consider additional measures to protect your code when writing in C. This becomes a problem especially when you consider how many hackers attempt to steal source codes and patented information. As a result, there are experts who fault the feasibility of C as a robust programming language when it comes to solving modern problems.

Code written in C is not reusable. This is a problem especially for programmers who learn in an open-source environment. Open-source learning encourages programmers to share knowledge and information with one another in the process of improving their skills and coming closer to creating amazing projects that can solve some of the glaring issues we have in the world of technology.

You have to be very patient when coding in C. The reason for this is because it is a very low-level abstraction language. It has maintained this feature since inception, even with advancements over the years. Bearing this in mind, and the fact that you have probably come across simpler and easier languages that deliver instant results, C is considerably limited. You will hardly ever get immediate results when using C, which is a big problem for many developers. Patience is everything in programming, but programming in C can push your limits.

There are a lot of object-oriented programming features that are not supported in C. This is quite a challenge for many programmers. Think about encapsulation, inheritance or even polymorphism. These features are not supported in C. It is actually in light of this that C++ came about. Beyond this, when writing code in C, you will also realize that type checking is not strict, which might be a problem for very specific values. When coding in C, it is easy to use a floating data type in place of an integer value.

When programming in C, one of the challenges you will experience is the inability to use namespace. Why is this a challenge? If you cannot use namespace, you will be unable to declare two variables that share a name. Other than that, you will also be unable to use that variable in the same concept.

For a language that is the building block of many other languages in use today, the fact that C does not perform runtime checking is a bother to many programmers. You can only perform time type checking at runtime. The problem here is that you will be unable to determine whether you are using the correct data type or not.

C compilers are unable to detect some errors. As a result, your program will probably run even with some errors that could easily have been detected in other languages. For example, when programming in C, a semicolon at the end of your loop could have two possibilities, either terminating the loop inadvertently or keep it running infinitely. Since the compilers have a high tolerance for errors, it might be difficult for you to determine the explanation behind some of the errors you experience.

Chapter 4:

C++ Programming

C++ is another general-purpose cross-platform programming language you will learn as you master programming. Having learned about C, C++ should be easier for you because the two languages share a lot of similarities. In fact, you can compile most of the programs written in C in C++ without altering the source code.

In as far as object-oriented programming is concerned, however, C++ is a safer language compared to C, and it features a better structure. Many programmers enjoy working with C++ because it was basically written as a utility language. Most of the other languages are created with a specific purpose in mind.

Given the insane number of programming languages available today, it is wise to choose a language depending on your needs and perspective of the project you are working on. While you can write some or many programs in C++, it might not be feasible considering the amount of time you have to spend on the task. This is why you must evaluate all the necessary conditions before you begin.

Assuming you are to write a program that has several GUI elements, it makes sense to use Python or Visual Basic since they come with the necessary GUI elements preinstalled. C++ plays an important role in many of the systems and applications we use today, including the following:

- Web frameworks and applications like .NET

- Web browsers

- Virtual machines

C++ allows users a very high level of control, especially with respect to system memory and resources in the process reducing the cost concerns in development. It is a portable language, and the applications written in C++ can be used in several platforms with ease.

Before you start writing code in C++, you must have a compiler and a text editor. There are several professional text editors available, but it is advisable that you use Notepad or whichever of the indigenous text editors that come preinstalled on your operating system.

You will also need an integrated development environment (IDE) within which you will compile and edit your C++ code. Some of the best options include Visual Studio, Eclipse and Blocks.

The following is a simple C++ code we will use to understand the foundations of this language:

```
#include <iostream>
using namespace std;

int main() {
  cout << "Welcome to my World!";
  return 0;
}
```

#include <iostream> allows us to introduce input and output objects.

using namespace std means that we can use the standard library for the names of variables and objects in use.

int main () refers to a function. This function executes any code that is written within the curly brackets.

cout refers to the print text or output used in the code. It is pronounced as see-out.

It is important to note that each C++ statement must end in a semicolon (;).

When writing code in C++, it is wise to remember that white spaces are ignored altogether. While you can write the code in one line, it is recommended that you break down the code into several lines so that it is easier to read.

return 0 is the end of the main function.

Output

Once you write the code correctly, *cout* alongside the << operator prints the desired output as shown below:

```
#include <iostream>

using namespace std;


int main() {

  cout << "Welcome to my World!";

  return 0;

}
```

It is possible to use as many outputs as possible as shown below:

```
#include <iostream>

using namespace std;


int main() {

  cout << "Welcome to my World!";

  cout << "This is my first piece";
```

```
  return 0;

}
```

You can add a new line to your code by inserting the \n character as shown:

```
#include <iostream>

using namespace std;


int main() {

  cout << "Welcome to my World! \n";

  cout << "This is my first piece";

  return 0;

}
```

Alternatively, you can use the *endl* manipulator to add a new line as shown:

```
#include <iostream>

using namespace std;


int main() {
```

```cpp
cout << "Welcome to my World!" <<endl;

cout << "This is my first piece";

return 0;

}
```

Comments in C++

Like we mentioned in C, you can use comments in C++ to help other developers understand your code and make it easier to read. You can either have the comments in a single line or multiple lines. The compiler ignores comments when executing code. Single line comments begin with two forward slashes (//) as shown below:

```cpp
// These are my personal views

cout << "Welcome to my World";
```

Multi-line comments begin with /* and end with */. Compilers will ignore all text within this construct. An example is shown below:

```cpp
/* These are my personal views*/

cout << "Hello World";
```

Variables in C++

Variables are storage containers holding different data values. The following are the types of variables that are used in C++:

- bool – for true or false values

- string – for text. They must be enclosed inside double quotes, for example *"Welcome home";*

- double – for floating numbers with decimals, like 25.36

- char – for single characters. They must be enclosed inside single quotes, for example 'd'

- int – for storing whole numbers that do not have decimals

When writing floating point numbers, you can use scientific numbers to define them, especially when using powers (e as a power of 10) as shown below:

> float f1 = 25e4;
>
> double d1 = 18e5;

cout << f1;

cout << d1;

All variables must be typified and have a value attached to them. The basic construct for this principle is as follows:

type variable = value;

For example:

int myNum = 18;

cout << myNum;

The C++ variables can be displayed as follows:

int myNum = 18;   // Integer

double myFloatNum = 35.67;   //   Floating
point number

char myLetter = 'T';   // Character

string myText = "Giver";   // String

bool myBoolean = false;   // Boolean

You can choose to add different variables together as shown below:

#include <iostream>

using namespace std;

```cpp
int main() {

int x = 10;

int y = 5;

int sum = x + y;

cout << sum;

return 0;

}
```

To declare more than two variables, the executable part of your code will be as follows:

```cpp
int x = 10, y = 5, z = 20;

cout << x + y + z;
```

Identifiers in C++

When using variables in C++, you must assign them unique names. These are the identifiers. You can use descriptive identifiers like age and height or short identifiers as used in the examples above like x, y and z.

When using identifiers in C++ most of the instructions in C apply. These are the terms you have to remember:

- Identifier names must use only underscores, digits and letters

- Identifier names can only start with an underscore or a letter

- Identifier names are case sensitive

- You must never use special characters or whitespaces in identifiers

- You cannot use special C++ keywords as identifiers

While *cout* is used with the insertion operator << to represent print values, we use *cin (pronounced see-in)* in C++ to represent input, using the extraction operator >> as shown below:

```
#include <iostream>

Usingnamespace std;


int main () {

int x, y;
int sum;
cout << "Enter a number: ";
```

```cpp
cin >> x;
cout << "Enter another number: ";
cin >> y;
sum = x + y;
cout << "Sum is: " << sum;

return 0;

}
```

Operators in C++

The role of an operator is to handle the operations applied to values and variables in the code. The operand is the value, while the operator refers to the operation that takes place between the operands. For example:

$$200 + 100$$

In the example above, *200* and *100* are the operands, while + is the operator.

Operators can be used with values as shown above. However, you can also use them to add variables and other variables or values as shown below:

```cpp
int sum1 = 200 + 100;      // 300  (200 + 100)

int sum2 = sum1 + 250;     // 550 (300 + 250)
```

int sum3 = sum2 + sum2;   // 1100 (550 + 550)

There are different kinds of operators used, grouped accordingly as follows:

- Arithmetic operators

These operators are used when performing the normal math operations, and include addition, division, modulus, multiplication, subtraction, decrement and increment.

- Logical operators

These operators institute logic between values or variables in use. They include *&&* (logical and), *!* (logical not) and || (logical or).

- Assignment operators

These operators bestow value upon variables. In the example below, the assignment operator (=) assigns the value *15* to the variable *y*:

int y = 15;

- Comparison operators

These operators compare different values. They include:

==   Equal to

!=   Not equal

<=	Less than or equal to
>=	Greater than or equal to
<	Less than
>	Greater than

C++ Strings

The purpose of strings in C++ is to store text. Strings are enclosed in double quotes as shown:

string greeting = "Howdy";

Before you use strings in C++, you have to declare the string in the header of your source code as shown:

// Include the string library

#include <string>

// Create a string variable

string greeting = "Howdy";

A concatenation is used to create a new string by adding together two strings as shown below:

```
string firstName = "Peter ";

string lastName = "Pan";

string fullName = firstName + lastName;

cout << fullName;
```

If you need to view the string entered by any of the users, you can use an extraction operator in the input as shown:

```
string firstName;
cout << "Enter full name: ";
cin >> firstName;      // obtain user input from
keyboard
cout << "Your Names are: " << firstName;
```

```
// Type your first name: Peter
// Your name is: Peter
```

Take note that *cin* will always consider space as a character terminating. Therefore, tabs, whitespace and so forth will be disregarded and the code will only show one word, irrespective of the number of words you enter.

In the example above, if the user entered *Peter Pan* as their full name, the code would only return *Peter* and ignore *Pan*.

To mitigate this problem, it is wise to use the function *getline ()* to read through the entire line of text. When you do this your code will recognize *cin* and the variable following it as the second parameter as shown below:

```
string fullName;
cout << "Enter full name: ";
getline (cin, fullName);
cout << "Your Names are: " << fullName;
```

```
// Type your full name: Peter Pan
// Your name is: Peter Pan
```

Performing Mathematical Operations in C++

There are several functions you can use in C++ to carry out mathematical tasks. Before you begin you have to declare *<cmath>* library in the header of your code as shown:

```
// Include the cmath library
```

```
#include <cmath>
```

Once you declare the math library, you can then proceed and indicate the mathematical functions applicable to your equation as shown below:

// Include the cmath library

#include <cmath>

cout << round (3.6);

cout << sqrt (9);

There are many other mathematical functions that are present in the <cmath library>, including the following:

- exp (x) – gives the value of E^x

- cosh (x) – gives the radian cosine value of x

- floor (x) – rounds off the value of x to the closest integer

- abs (x) – gives an absolute value of x

Boolean Expressions in C++

In many cases you will come across some data that only have predefined values, like true or false, on and off, yes or no. This is the *bool* data type in C++. True values take *(1)* while false values take *(0)*.

Boolean expressions are shown as follows:

```cpp
bool isFootballExciting = true;
bool isCornTasty = false;
cout << isFootballExciting;  // Outputs 1 (true)
cout << isCornTasty;  // Outputs 0 (false)
```

While the convention is to read the Boolean expressions as *1* and *0* values, they can also be expressed in Boolean values using operators as shown:

```cpp
int x                                    = 21;
int y                                    = 13;
cout << (x > y); // returns 1 (true), because 21 is greater than 13
```

The expression above can also be represented as follows:

```cpp
cout << (21 > 13); // returns 1 (true), because 21 is greater than 13
```

```cpp
int x = 21;
```

```cpp
cout << (x == 21); // returns 1 (true), because x is equal to 21
```

```cpp
cout << (21== 13); // returns 0 (false), because 21 is not equal to 13
```

It is important to understand Boolean expressions because they are the foundation of operations and comparisons in C++.

If Statements and Conditions

In C++ the normal mathematical conditions are used when applying logic as follows:

- x < y (less than)

- x > y (greater than)

- x <= y (less than or equal to)

- x >=y (greater than or equal to)

- x == y (equal to)

- x != y (not equal to)

In decision making, the following rules apply when using if and else statements in C++:

- if – when a given condition is true of the code you want to execute

- else – when a given condition is false of the code you want to execute

- switch – identify a different set of code to run

- else if – identify a new condition to run if the first one is false

Let's look at some examples below:

The if statement

```cpp
if (88 > 8) {
  cout << "88 is greater than 8";
}
```

```cpp
int x = 88;
int y = 8;
if (x > y) {
  cout << "x is greater than y";
}
```

The else statement

```cpp
int time = 11;
if (time < 17) {
  cout << "Good morning.";
} else {
  cout << "Good evening.";
}
// Outputs "Good morning."
```

The else-if statement

```cpp
int time = 20;
if (time < 11) {
  cout << "Good morning.";
} else if (time < 18) {
  cout << "Good day.";
```

```
} else {
  cout << "Good evening.";
}
// Outputs "Good evening."
```

The switch statement

This statement allows you to choose a single block of code to run from several available. It is expressed in the following syntax:

```
switch(expression) {
  case a:
    // code block
    break;
  case b:
    // code block
    break;
  default:
    // code block
}
```

The *switch* expression is registered when you run the code. It compares all the values in the cases available and will only execute the case whose values match.

Let's look at an example that uses the number assigned to calendar months to output the month of the year below:

```cpp
int month = 5;
switch (month) {
  case 1:
   cout << "January";
   break;
  case 2:
   cout << "February";
   break;
  case 3:
   cout << "March";
   break;
  case 4:
   cout << "April";
   break;
  case 5:
   cout << "May";
   break;
  case 6:
   cout << "June";
   break;
  case 7:
   cout << "July";
   break;
}
// Outputs "May" (month 5)
```

What is the role of a *break* in this code? *Break* is a keyword used in C++ to stop the block from executing the code when it finds a match. At this point, there is no use in consuming more resources to keep testing when the right answer has been found.

Default is a keyword that is used to indicate specific code in case the test does not reveal a match. For example:

```
int month = 9;
switch (month) {
 case 1:
  cout << "January";
  break;
 case 2:
  cout << "February";
  break;
 case 3:
  cout << "March";
  break;
 case 4:
  cout << "April";
  break;
 case 5:
  cout << "May";
  break;
 case 6:
  cout << "June";
  break;
 case 7:
  cout << "July";
  break;

default:

cout <<"No space available, come back next year";
}
// Outputs "No space available, come back next year"
```

Possible Challenges When Programming in C++

In as far as efficient programming languages are concerned, C++ is one of the languages that you should strongly consider. So many years have gone by since its inception, though it is still a dominant force, and a lot of programmers are learning it with ease.

As a beginner, it is wise to know what to expect when using C++, especially since you might have learned other languages too. Here are some of the challenges you might experience:

When programming in C++, you might realize that your programs keep crashing a lot. Other than crashing, there are many instances where you have anomalous behavior when coding. One of the reasons for this is that it is difficult for a lot of beginner programmers to understand the concept of pointers. Other than that, the use of pointers is resource intensive, so you might also experience lags in performance.

C++ was introduced, among other reasons, to solve some of the inherent problems that programmers had experienced in C. One of the glaring issues in C is security. While C++ made attempts to deal with this, it is not effective. When programming, especially for object-oriented programming, data security is one of the most important issues you cannot ever take lightly.

Some of the issues you will experience with C++, in as far as security is concerned, include pointers, global variables and problems using some functions.

You will have to learn a lot of C++ on your own. This is one of those caveats that many beginner programmers never realize. Learning institutions hardly ever teach C++, and the few that have instructors do not go as deep as they should. However, there is a workaround for this. If you have a good instructor for C or any of the other languages, you can leverage that knowledge and use it to learn C++ in your spare time.

It is quite unfortunate that most institutions do not teach C++ or give it the attention it deserves. It gets worse because C++ is notoriously known to be a difficult language to learn. Of course, you will come across simpler ways to learn C++, but in general the concepts you have to master in C++ are relatively difficult, which can put you off, especially if you have had access to simpler languages before.

C++ is not independent. As an improvement of C, a lot of the hardware, interfaces and structure in C++ is borrowed from C. Therefore, to learn and master C++, you have to go out of your way and learn C. This can be time consuming. However, the time spent learning C to improve your understanding of C++ does not go to waste. Since you will be working with different operating systems, this is basic and critical knowledge. All the operating systems are written in C after all. So, the way things look, you cannot avoid learning C.

Error handling in C++ is ambiguous and frustrating. The reason for this is because the compilers used in C++ are notorious for returning very long error messages which are also difficult to read. For you to understand the error message, you must have in-depth knowledge to have a shot at sorting the errors out. Otherwise, most of your projects will be loaded with errors, many of which you will never detect.

When using C++ for web applications, you will have a difficult time debugging errors. C++ is not exactly the best language to use for apps that are platform specific. Some applications are specifically designed to run on Windows or Mac. As a result, they come with an inherent library, which makes your work difficult when debugging web applications. It might actually be impossible to do so.

Chapter 5:

C# Programming

C# (C Sharp) is a programming language created by Microsoft. It is an object-oriented programming language intended for general purposes. While Microsoft built C# to help developers work with their .Net framework, there are several amazing features built into the programming language which have made it a mainstay in the world of programming and helped design many applications over the years.

Most of the features of C# are similar to C and C++, so prior knowledge of these two might help you learn C# faster. The design of the C# language was aimed at helping developers work around computational complexities in their models, and through the .Net framework they can use the command line interface (CLI) to write and execute code.

The following are some of the applications that have been built with C#:

- Malware and virus

- Database applications

- Applications running on Windows

- GUI based applications

- Web applications

- Desktop software

- Distributed applications

In as much as there are lots of programming languages available today, developers are still encouraged to learn C#, being that it is one of the fundamental languages behind a lot of the programs, apps and systems that you will come across in your programming career.

C# is also one of the easiest languages to learn. This, coupled with the fact that it is a general-purpose language, allows you to integrate it into any other programming language that you have mastery of. Programs written in C# can easily be read on other machines because of this.

By design, C# is a well-structured language. There are conventions and instructions that, when followed accordingly, allow programmers to implement their projects and concepts without a lot of problems. Towards this end, programmers can also leverage the independence of C# when writing code, because the underlying programs can be executed without any issues in most of the computing environments being used at the moment.

The popularity and efficiency of C# comes down to the following reasons:

- Programmers can use Lambda and LINQ expressions in their work

- C# supports the use of generic concepts

- When coding in C#, you can use indexers and the language also allows multi-threading

- Garbage collections in C# are automated

- There are several standard libraries built into C#

- C# has in-built events and properties that encourage smart programming

Structure of C# Program

It is important to understand the basic construct of a program written in C#. With this information, you will be in a good position to understand the syntax and architecture you come across. The following is an example of a simple program written in C#:

```
using System;

namespace printHelloCsharp

{

  class HelloCsharp {
```

```
static void Main(string[] args)

{

  /* Print some string in C# */

  Console.WriteLine("Welcome to C#.");

  Console.ReadKey();

  }

 }

}
```

Output

Welcome to C#

From the program above, we can identify the following key elements:

- *using* – fetches any methods associated with the namespace

- *Namespace* – declares a collection of classes in one unit

- *main()* – different methods for calling variables

- */*Comments*/* - comments are used to enhance users' understanding of the code, and are not read by the compiler

- *Class* – maintains the concept

- *Console.WriteLine()* – shows the variables and strings in the program

- *Console.ReadKey()* – informs the program to wait for user input

Variables

Every programming language has specific instructions that programmers must follow to write and execute code. These instructions concern the way data is stored and handled in the language. Some of the most important instructions concern variables and how to assign values to the variables in question. A variable can be used several times in the program and can also be changed accordingly.

The following are the basic variables you will use in C#:

- Nullable variables

- Boolean variables

- Decimal variables

- Floating type variables

- Integer variables

Before using a variable in C#, you must define it properly. The syntax for defining programs in C# is as follows:

<data_type> <variable_names>;

For example:

int d, b, e

Variables in C# are initialized when you use an assignment operator *(=)*. Following the syntax above, the initiated variable is as shown below:

<data_type> <variable_name> = value;

For example:

int xy = 8, roll = 48

char ch = 'h'

Programs written in C# have the function *Readline()*. This function stores user input in variables as shown below:

double sal;

```
sal = Convert.ToDouble(Console.ReadLine());
```

From this example, we can reveal from the first line that we are dealing with a double type variable. In the next line, once the user keys in the data, the program will convert it into the double data type through the *Convert.ToDouble()* and deliver a *sal* variable.

Data Types in C#

Declaring data types before you input the variable informs the compiler of the type of data it will handle and the variables to which the data will be assigned for storage. This is a concept that cuts across C, C++, C# and almost all the programming languages you will come across.

There are three types of variables in C#:

- Value

- Reference

- Pointer

Value type variables

Value type variables are those that have values assigned to them directly. They are found in the *System.ValueType* class. In this category, we have the following types of data:

Integral type

C# allows for up to eight integral definitions. They all support 64-bit, 32-bit and 8-bit values, irrespective of whether their modifiers are signed or not. The eight definitions are:

- short

- sbyte

- int

- long

- byte

- ushort

- uint

- ulong

Floating type

There are two types of floating-point data types in C#, 64-bit and 32-bit.

64-bit floating point types contain 14-15 digits and must be declared with the keyword *double*. When writing the value, you must declare a *d* or *D* at the end of the value as shown below:

double ks = 8.274925d

32-bit floating point types contain seven digits and must be declared with the keyword *float*. When writing the value, you must declare an *f* or *F* at the end of the value as shown below:

$$\text{float } g = 46.2f$$

It is important to remember the suffix *f*, because without it compilers will assume you input a double value and treat it as a 64-bit value.

Decimal type

In case you are working with calculations that demand 128-bit computations, especially for large data, decimal type variables are used. The suffix for such variables is an *M*, without which the compiler will assume a double variable.

Character type

These variables store single characters in a 16-bit Unicode format.

Reference type variables

The major difference between reference type variables and the other kinds of variables is that instead of storing the real data, they store a reference to the data in question. Therefore, reference type variables point to specific memory locations. The following are the reference types you will come across in C#:

- Object data type

- String data type

- Dynamic data type

Pointer type variables

Pointers hold addresses of the locations of other types of data. They are represented as follows:

type* identifier;

For example

int* user_id

Keywords in C#

There are several keywords and features in C# that make it one of the best languages programmers use today. This wealth of resources also makes C# a versatile language for different tasks.

Following the same convention in C and C++, keywords in C# cannot be used as identifiers. This is because keywords have unique roles in the inherent language and for this reason compilers have special instructions on how they are defined.

The following are the types of keywords used in C#:

- Query keywords (descending, ascending, group, where, from, let, join, select, into)

- Type keywords (ushort, ulong, long, short, sbyte, bool, byte, struct, double, decimal, class, uint)

- Contextual keywords (value, set, dynamic, var, add, global)

- Literal keywords (void, value, true, false, null)

- Operator keywords (checked, unchecked, new, is, await, as, typeof, stackalloc)

- Access keywords (this, base)

- Namespace keywords (extern alias, .operator, using, :: operator)

- Method parameter keywords (out, ref, params)

- Statement keywords (finally, continue, if, else, default, for, do, case, while, in, return, break)

- Modifier keywords (volatile, event, static, sealed, partial, override, new, const)

- Access modifier keywords (internal, protected, private, public)

Operators

The role of operators is in mathematical computations. They are symbols that instruct the compiler on how to handle operations and deliver the desired output. C# has the following types of operators:

Arithmetic operators

They are used in computations that demand mathematical or increase/decrease operations. They include:

- Decrement –
- Increment++
- Modulus %
- Division /
- Addition +
- Multiplication *
- Subtraction -

Relational operators

The role of these operators is to compare the relationship between two operands. They include:

- Greater than >

- Less than <

- Equal to ==

- Not equal to !=

- Greater than equal to >=

- Less than equal to <=

Logical operators

The role of these operators is to derive a logical decision from more than two conditions. The operators are as follows:

- Logical NOT (!) which is true if the desired conditions are met

- Logical OR (||) which is true if one or all conditions are met

- Logical AND (&&) which is true if both conditions are met

Bitwise operators

These operations run bit by bit operations at the bit level and include the following:

- Bitwise Right Shift >>

- Bitwise Left Shift <<

- Bitwise XOR ^

- Bitwise OR |

- Bitwise AND &

Assignment operators

Their function is to apportion values to operations being executed. They include the following:

- |=

- ^=

- &=

- >>=

- <<=

- %=

- /=

- *=

- -=

- +=

- =

The operators above first handle the left side of the operator, then the right side and finally assigns the variable to the left.

Miscellaneous operators

These operators can be used in different scenarios whenever applicable. They include:

- is

- Conditional operator (?)

- Address of operator (&)

- typeof()

- sizeof

- Pointer to variable operator (*)

Decision Making in C#

Decision making in C# helps programmers understand whether the conditions outlined are met when they run the program. Some instructions are only performed when the conditions outlined for them are met.

The following are the decision-making statements used in C#:

- If

This statement confirms whether the conditions are true. If true, the block of code is executed.

The syntax for if statements is as shown below:

if (condition)

{

//execute code

}

- If-else

This statement confirms whether the conditions are true. If true, the block of code is executed. If the conditions are not true, the code defined by the *else* statement is executed. Basically, it provides an alternative. The syntax is as follows:

if(condition)

{

// if condition is true

}

else

{

// if the condition is false

}

• If-else-if

This statement executes a defined block of code by analyzing a specific condition from different conditional statements. It reviews all the statements and executes the condition whose statement is true. The syntax is shown below:

if(first-condition) {

// when first condition is true

}

else if(second-condition)

{

// when second condition is true

}

else if(third-condition)

{

// when third condition is true

}

else

```
{
```

// when all are false

```
}
```

- **Nested if**

This statement involves one if statement inside another if or else statement. You have to evaluate different conditions and ensure they are true before the nested conditional statements are performed. The syntax is as follows:

if (first-condition)

```
{
```

// when first condition is true

if (second-condition)

```
{
```

// execute the code

// if second condition is true

```
}
```

```
}
```

- **Switch**

You can use a *switch* statement instead of the *if-else-if* statement. The compiler checks the code in an expression to determine whether it matches the desired case. Every block of code exits when the case is matched, so the program does not have to keep running or search through additional blocks of code. The syntax is as follows:

```
switch (expression)

{

case 1:// statements

break;


case 2:// statements

break;


case N:// statements

break;

default:// default statements

}
```

Loops in C#

The concept of loops is about repetitive tasks. There are some tasks that have to be performed all the time. This can be time-consuming, chaotic and hectic in programming. It also increases the risk of errors.

Loops are used in programming languages to execute specific statements a given number of times if they meet specific conditions. There are two types of loops in C#:

- Entry controlled loops

In a controlled loop, the condition is verified at the beginning of the loop before the code is executed. There are two types of entry-controlled loops: *while loop* and *for loop*.

While loop conditions will persist up to the point where the condition is false. The syntax is as follows:

while (boolean conditions)

{

// loop statements

}

For example:

```csharp
using System;

class IterateWithWhile

{
    public static void Main()

    {
        int cntr = 1;

        while (cntr <= 4)

        {
            Console.WriteLine(" Welcome Home "+cntr);

            cntr++;

        }

    }

}
```

Output:

Welcome Home 1

Welcome Home 2

Welcome Home 3

Welcome Home 4

For loops check the condition of the loop against a counter variable. It performs an increment or decrement before separating the expressions with a semicolon as shown below:

for (introduce counter variable; test loop condition; increment / decrement)

{

// loop statements

}

For example:

```
using System;

class IterationWithFor

{

    public static void Main()

    {

        for (int cntr = 1; cntr <= 4; cntr++)

            Console.WriteLine(" Welcome Home "+cntr);

    }
```

}

Output:

Welcome Home 1

Welcome Home 2

Welcome Home 3

Welcome Home 4

- **Exit controlled loops**

Exit controlled loops verify the condition in the body of the statement and at the end of the code. In C#, the *do-while* loop is the only exit controlled loop statement available. It works in the same way as the while loop, only that it verifies the condition of the code at the end instead of the beginning. Therefore, whether the predefined condition is met or not, the loop will still be executed.

The syntax is as follows:

do

{

// loop statements

} while (condition);

Here's an example:

```
using System;

class IterateWithDoWhile

{

    public static void Main()

    {

        int cntr = 9;

        do

        {

            Console.WriteLine(" Welcome Home "+cntr);

            cntr++;

        }

        while (cntr < 8);

    }

}
```

Output:

Welcome Home 9

Infinite Loops

In some cases, you can come across a loop whose condition will never be false. For this reason, the loop will persist until it is terminated externally. These are infinite loops.

Possible Challenges When Programming in C#

Programming in C# has its perks, especially when you compare it against the likes of C and C++. At some point you might have to consider switching from another language to C# and it would be wise to have all the necessary information.

In light of this, learning about the possible challenges when using C# will help you prepare accordingly. The following are some of the issues you should be psychologically prepared for when programming in C#.

One of the biggest issues you will have with C# is beyond your control—Microsoft! Over the years, many tech companies stop supporting older variants of their programs in a bid to encourage their users to move to the latest versions. Perhaps the older version works for you for a specific reason and an upgrade would not suit your immediate needs.

When programming in C#, you can expect discontinued support for older .NET frameworks over time. This usually happens once Microsoft upgrades or updates their operating systems after a while. To continue coding in C#, therefore, you would have to upgrade to a newer machine or a new operating system.

There are solid arguments in favor of upgrading your system. However, upgrades usually come with unique challenges that even some of the top programmers in the world struggle to get around. This also explains why many companies prefer to keep the old reliable versions that they have instead of upgrading. Think in terms of the architectural upgrade, the training and the cost in terms of innocent errors that users will make before they get accustomed to the system.

Another challenge you will experience when running C# is the type of server. C# runs on the .NET framework. Therefore, it must run on a Windows server. The problem comes in when you use a Linux server, as many organizations prefer. For personal use at home, you might be okay with C# as it is. If you think about the office scenario, Windows hosting is your best option.

The problem with Windows hosting is that it is considerably expensive compared to Linux server hosting. You might have a difficult time explaining to your account managers why you need an upgrade, especially if they don't understand a thing about technology.

C# is a very buggy language. This comes from the need to compile code all the time. Of course, compiling code is a good thing. However, doing it all the time creates a problem. Working with C# is not easy because you have to keep compiling code every time you alter the code. Even with the slightest change in code, it has to be compiled again.

It is so petty that you must compile the code even after you change a single letter in it. After that, you have to compile the entire program before you execute it. It can be so frustrating, and in the process, you end up with a buggy code especially if you did not test the changes accordingly.

Are you a beginner in programming? Well, C# is probably not the best place for you to start. You are better off learning other languages first, then graduating to C#. It is advisable that you learn other languages like VB.Net or C first, master the concepts and syntax before you go to C#. The syntax used in C# is complex, and you could easily be dissuaded from learning if you run into problems from the very beginning.

One thing you must do in C#, which you don't necessarily have to in other languages, is to use a semicolon at the end of your code. This is a convention that you get used to from practice, but it might weigh down on you. If you work with different languages at the same time, it might also be quite confusing.

Case sensitivity in C# is another issue you must remember. It is easy to confuse yourself or anyone who is reading your code when you use some variables interchangeably. By default, when you write username and UserName in C#, these are two different variables. If you don't stick to this convention, you will end up with errors because one variable will call different values and ignore the others.

From experience with other languages, there are some features in C# that you might feel should not be included, like override, properties and others that many programmers need to use in the course of their work, which are missing, like multiple inheritance.

C# is largely inflexible. Given that it depends on .NET to run, you will struggle to work with anything that is not featured on .NET or supported at all. Besides that, it is relatively slower to run C# than most of the other languages that you might come across. Many expert programmers do contend that it is very difficult to become a complete expert at C# because it has too many features, many of which you will hardly ever use.

Chapter 6:

Programming in Python

Python is one of the top languages currently used in object-oriented programming. Knowledge of Python today is important, especially considering the fact that it is the main language used in neural networks, artificial intelligence and so many other aspects of computer science that affect our lives directly.

Learning Python is easy, and you don't necessarily need prior programming knowledge. However, if you have learned other languages already, your grasp of Python will be easier and faster. The basic construct of a Python statement is that you must have brackets around the values you expect as output. This is shown below:

print ("Welcome Home")

Output:

Welcome Home

Python is a portable language and is preferred by most developers because its syntax is very easy to understand. For example, if we want to add two numbers, a simple Python program would read as follows:

```
x = y y = 10 #declare two variables and store 10 into
them
```

```
print (x + y) #final output
```

Output:

20

Why should you learn Python? Other than the fact that it is one of the most popular languages in the world at the moment, Python is a scalable language. Its structure can be enhanced to support projects of different sizes whenever applicable. Besides the scalability, the fact that it is an extendable language allows you to introduce other modules into the interpreter while writing your programs.

As long as the interface is similar, you can run Python code on different kinds of hardware. This portability, coupled with the fact that Python code is one of the easiest to read and understand, further explains why it is so popular today. The simplicity of the Python syntax is one of the reasons why it is so popular.

There is so much that you can do once you learn how to code in Python. Some of the top applications in use today that run on Python include YouTube and Instagram, which is proof that you can use Python to build some amazing projects.

Python interpreters are stored in a *.pyc* file. There are two modes in which you can use the interpreter, either in script mode or interactive mode.

In script mode, the source code is kept in a unique file with a *.py* extension. The interpreter will then read the content of the file and run the code. You must specify the location of the file for the interpreter to identify it and execute the code.

Assuming you are working on some code and save the file as *WelcomeHome.py*, you will write the following script in Python:

python WelcomeHome.py

In the interactive mode, you don't need to pass your script through an interpreter. Instead, you write the code and push it to the Python prompt as shown below:

>>> 5+5

Output:

10

The symbol >>> prompts the interpreter that you are ready for output.

Many programmers prefer interactive mode over script mode especially in scenarios where you are writing small fragments of code. This applies to code that is less than four lines. If your code is longer than this, script coding will be the best way.

Standard Data Types

Compared to most of the other programming languages, Python uses unique data types that are easy to comprehend and use. Since it is an interpreted language, the interpreter identifies the data type on its own, meaning that you no longer have to identify the memory location as you would with other programing languages.

Python data types help the interpreter figure out how to store values, the types of values, operations that you can perform with the data, and more importantly, to decipher the meaning of that data.

All objects in Python have unique values and data types. By design, Python accommodates numerous data types. The following are some of the most important ones which you will come across regularly:

- Sequences, including tuples, lists, strings and bytes

- Numbers

- Dictionaries

- Sets

- Boolean

- File

- Method

- Function

- Module

- Class

Strings

A string refers to a line of programming text that users can access. Everything in Python is an object, including strings. A string is any characters enclosed inside double quotes, as shown below:

var = "Welcome Home"

In Python, characters are not supported. As a result, all characters are considered as sub-strings. Below is an example of what strings look like on the screen:

ch = 'Welcome Home'

str1 = "Strings"

print ("Second value is: " , ch)

print ("Third value is: " , str1)

Output:

Second value is: Welcome Home

Third value is: Strings

It is easier to reassign or update a string in Python than other languages. All you need to do is to introduce the + operator as shown below:

ch = 'Welcome Home'

print ("Updated string will be:" , ch [:10]+ "Home")

Output:

Updated string will be Welcome HoHome

Python has unique characters that serve special roles, referred to as escape characters. These characters have a backslash ahead of them. To interpret them, you can either use a single or double quote. The Python escape characters are as follows:

- \v – vertical tab

- \t – tab

- \s – space

- \r – carriage return

- \n – next line

- \f – form feed

- \e - escape

- \cx – control x

- \b – backspace

- \a – alert

Repeat strings

While writing code, you might have to repeat a given string a number of times. Instead of writing it over and over, you can simply use the repetition operator (*), as shown below:

str = 'Welcome Home'

print (str*3)

Output:

Welcome HomeWelcome HomeWelcome Home

You can also repeat only a specific part of the string, as follows:

str = 'Welcome Home'

print (str[3:5]*3) #This will repeat the third and fourth character

Output:

lclclc

We mentioned earlier that everything in Python is considered an object. On the same note, Python assumes spaces are characters in the string. Therefore, it is important that you get rid of them, because spaces in the wrong place might interfere with the execution of your code.

The following is an example of how this becomes a problem: If you write *'Welcome '* instead of *'Welcome'*, the string will deliver an error as shown below:

if 'Welcome' == 'Welcome ':

print ("Welcome Home!")

else:

print ("Not found")

Based on this convention, it is impossible to output the right data. This is why your code might not execute at all. So, before executing your string you must get rid of all the blank spaces.

You can delete blank spaces in any of the following methods:

- *strip()* – deletes spaces at both ends of your string

- *lstrip()* – deletes spaces at the beginning of your string

- *rstrip()* – deletes spaces at the end of your string

Take note that none of these methods will delete empty spaces inside the string, but just at the ends. They can be used as follows:

name = ' Welcome Home '

#remove spaces from left

print (name.lstrip())

#remove spaces from right

print (name.rstrip())

#remove spaces from both side

print (name.strip())

It is easy to update your strings in Python by updating the old one with a new one. The new value is associated with the old value or a new string. The string *replace()* method delivers the same string, but with new values as shown:

oldstring = 'Welcome Home'

newstring = oldstring.replace('Home' , 'Back')

Output:

Welcome Back

Lists

Without a proper convention, dealing with data can be difficult. In Python, you can use lists and tuples to organize data into sets that are easy to manage. There are different sequences under which data can be organized.

Lists are simply containers. They store some information in a specific order. Lists have a predefined sequence that determine how information is stored, and developers can then remove or add more items to the list according to the sequence. All items in the sequence are identifiable by a number assigned to them.

Creating lists in Python is as simple as enclosing some data in square brackets *[]* as shown below:

lst1 = []

lst2 = [expression1, expression2, expression3, ...]

For example

lst1 = ['math', 'science', 'history']

lst2 = [2012, 2013, 2014]

lst3 = [4, 6, 8, "r", "s" "k"]

To access the items in your lists, the following rules apply:

- *l* – queries the number of items contained in the list

- *l(k)* – queries the item represented by index number k

- *l(k:m)* – queries the list of items within objects k and m

To access the lists above, the following code applies:

lst1 = ['math', 'science', 'history']

lst2 = [2012, 2013, 2014]

lst3 = [4, 6, 8, "r", "s" "k"]

print ("lst1[0]", lst1 [0])

print ("lst3[2:4]", lst3[2:4])

Output:

lst1[0] math

lst3[2:4] [8, "r"]

You can add one or more items to your list above as shown below:

lst1 = ['math', 'science', 'history']

print ("Third item on the list is:")

print (lst1[1])

lst1[1] = Music

print ("Updated value in the third index of list is:")

print (lst1[1])

Output:

Third item on the list is:

history

Updated value in the third index of list is:

Music

In case you need to delete some values from your list, the *del-statement* syntax below will help:

del list_name[index_val];

Tuples

A tuple in Python refers to a list whose content is fixed and cannot be changed from the moment it is created. The following conditions apply to tuples:

- Their elements have a defined order

- Instead of square braces, tuples are contained in parentheses

- They share similar definitions with lists

The following syntax shows how to access values in tuples:

tupl1 = ('math', 'science', 'history');

tupl2 = (2012, 2013, 2014);

tupl3 = (12, 14, 16, 18);

print ("tupl1[0]", tupl1[0])

print ("tupl3[2:4]", tupl3[2:4])

Output:

tupl1[0] math

tupl3[2:4] (16, 18)

Given that tuples cannot be changed, the only way you can update them is if you join them together as shown below:

tupl1 = (4, 5, 6)

tupl2 = ('ba', 'dc')

tupl3 = (tupl1 + tupl2)

Output:

(4, 5, 6, 'ba', dc)

To delete a tuple the del-statement applies as shown below:

tupl2 = ('ba', 'dc')

del tupl2

Keywords

In the same way as other programming languages, keywords in Python cannot be used as variables or identifiers. They are specifically reserved for internal purposes. All Python keywords are written in small letters, and they are as follows:

- try

- lambda

- print

- class

- exec

- with

- or

- for

- import

- global

- elif

- except

- def

- return

- is

- yield

- break

- as

- while

- not

- if

- finally

- pass

- continue

- fron

- del

- assert

- in

- else

- raise

- and

Statements

Decision statements come into play when you write a program that can make specific choices regarding how to execute a block of code. Your program basically predicts what happens next if it executes the code or not.

Python uses the following decision statements:

- *if* – the statements result in true or false

if expression:

#run the code

Example:

x = 30

if x > 25

    print ("x is the greater")

Output:

x is the greater

- *if else* – the *else* statement is executed in case the if statement is false if expression:

#run the code

else

#run the code

Example:

x = 30

y = 45

if x > y:

print ("x is the greater")

else:

print ("y is the greater")

Output:

y is the greater

- nested statements – one or more if or if else statements can be performed within an if or if else statement.

elif statements are a replacement of the else if statement. They introduce new conditions within the program, hence their reference as chained conditionals.

Syntax:

```
if expression:

  #run the code

elif expression:

  #run the code

else:

  #run the code
```

Example:

```
x = 105

y = 105


if x > y:

  print("x is the greater")

elif x == y:

  print("both are equal")

else:

  print("y is greater")
```

Output:

both are equal

You can also have a condition within a single statement, especially if your statement only runs on one line as follows:

x = 20

if (x ==20): print('The value of x is 20')

Output:

The value of x is 20

Loops in Python

Loops in programming perform a given set of instructions a predetermined number of times or within a specific set of conditions. The code will keep running until those conditions are met. Instead of writing the same code all the time, you can create a loop to execute that code until the desired output is delivered. The following types of loops are used in Python:

- while loop – this loop persists until the code meets a given Boolean condition.

#initialize count variable to 11

count =11

while count < 16 :

   print (count)

   count+=1

#the line above means count = count + 1

Output:

11

12

13

14

15

- for loop – this loop persists until the code is run a given number of times

Example:

```
for x in range (0,3):

print ('Welcome Home %d' % (x))
```

Output:

Welcome Home 0

Welcome Home 1

Welcome Home 2

Example:

```
for letter in 'Welcome':

        print ('Current letter is:', letter)
```

Output:

Current letter is: W

Current letter is: e

Current letter is: l

Current letter is: c

Current letter is: o

Current letter is: m

Current letter is: e

- nested loop – this is a while or for loop that exists within another while or for loop

Example:

for x in range (3,8):

    for y in range (2,4):

        print ("%d * %d =%d" % (x, y, x*y))

Output:

3 * 2 = 6

3 * 3 = 9

4 * 2 = 8

4 * 3 = 12

5 * 2 = 10

5 * 3 = 15

6 * 2 = 12

6 * 3 = 18

7 * 2 = 14

7 * 3 = 21

Control Statements

The loop statement will proceed until it encounters a conditional statement that instructs it to change the sequence of execution. There are three control statements used in Python as shown in the examples below:

- **Break**

This statement instructs the program to terminate the loop and proceed with the next statement.

Example:

count = 20

while count <= 100: print (count) count += 1 if count >= break

Output:

20

21

22

- **Continue**

This statement skips the rest of the loop at the point it is encountered and begins retesting the loop.

Example:

```
for y in range(11):

    #check whether y is odd

    if y % 2 == 0:

        continue

    print (y)
```

Output:

2

4

6

8

10

- **Pass**

This statement applies when you don't need to execute any commands but need a syntactical statement from the string.

Example:

```
for letter in 'WelcomeHome':

    if letter == 'H':

        pass

        print ('Pass block')

    print ('Current letter is:', letter)
```

Output:

Current letter is: W

Current letter is: e

Current letter is: l

Current letter is: c

Current letter is: o

Current letter is: m

Current letter is: e

Pass block

Current letter is: H

Current letter is: o

Current letter is: m

Current letter is: e

Possible Challenges When Programming in Python

While Python is one of the most amazing languages you can program in, you have to be aware of what lies ahead. Each language has its unique challenges that you must be prepared for. Let's have a look at some of them.

One of the first issues you might have with Python, especially if you have written code before in C++ or C, is that it is a slow language. Compared to the two, Python is relatively slower. However, this is expected, given that it is a high-level language compared to the others. Therefore, Python is more of a software application language than C and C++, which are more inclined towards hardware.

While it is possible to experiment with Python on different projects, you might realize that it is not a very good language to use when you are programming projects for mobile development. This does not mean that you cannot use it. You can still code in Python, but you might have some challenges. Experts consider Python a weak language with respect to mobile app development, and this is one of the reasons why there are relatively limited mobile apps written in Python.

One of the issues that has been raised in the past by many programmers is that Python tends to be design flawed. As a result, you should expect to deal with a lot of runtime errors. The reason for this is because, primarily, Python is a dynamic language that has to be typed. It is easier for programmers to use because most of the code you write is in normal human language. Therefore, you must be ready to spend a lot of time testing code to make sure it runs properly. Even with that in mind, you will still encounter a number of errors during runtime, which you might never catch while testing the program.

In case your development resources are limited, you might struggle to appreciate the benefits of Python. The reason for this is because Python is a relatively resource-intensive language. If you have limited memory, it would be wise to invest in a new machine to help you code faster and with fewer frustrations. One of the main reasons for Python's insane resource consumption is because the data types used are very flexible.

Having used Python for a while, you will probably enjoy the flexibility in the library extensibility. This is something that most of the other programs do not have. Python allows you to extend libraries to the point where it almost feels you are speaking in normal language instead of computer languages. Because of this reason, a lot of programmers who spend a lot of time coding in Python eventually struggle to code in any of the other languages.

Another issue that you will realize when programming in Python is that the database access layers have not undergone serious development over the years. This is especially true when you compare other technologies like ODBC. If you have used any of the other access layers before, you might find Python's access layer a primitive and difficult to work with.

Having considered all the challenges above, Python is still one of the best programming languages you can learn. Coding in Python is probably easier than most of the popular languages because it is as close to normal human language as possible, which makes it easy to understand.

Chapter 7:

Programming in JavaScript

JavaScript is an open source scripting language that is used in web browsers. The primary role of JavaScript is to improve user interaction with websites; hence it is a client-side language.

JavaScript works through engines. While the operation of the engines might be complicated, the script follows a simple three-step process. The engine parses the script, converts it to a language the machine can understand and then the machine executes the code.

There are several reasons why you should consider learning JavaScript. Today user experience is more important than ever on the internet. For this reason, webmasters must make sure their websites are appealing to their audiences and, more importantly, meets their needs. To do this, they have to create dynamic websites. It is through JavaScript that users can interact with the dynamic content on websites.

JavaScript also allows users to interact with the websites on a higher level. It is because of JavaScript that the browser can detect mouse clicks, movements of your pointer, and any activity you perform on the keyboard.

JavaScript also enables you to retrieve data from the website and download it to your storage devices, view messages, switch from one window or tab to the other, play media files and so many other activities you need to interact with the browser.

JavaScript stands out as a unique language, especially in comparison to any of the other languages that you can use. With JavaScript, you can build a website that has fully integrated CSS and HTML, allowing you to perform tasks faster without going through a lot of conventions.

JavaScript supports many other script languages that are available today. If you write code in any language like Dart, you can simply convert it to JavaScript and run it. Besides, the most popular browsers today all support JavaScript by default.

As a developer, especially if you plan to venture into web and app development, you should be adept in CSS, HTML and JavaScript. Other than websites, JavaScript is also used in developing games and mobile apps.

Most of the syntax used in JavaScript is borrowed from C programming. JavaScript is a scripting language, which means it is impossible to run it independently. Your web browser is built to run the JavaScript scripts.

To learn the basics of JavaScript programming, you will use the native text editor that comes with your operating system and your preferred browser to test your code. As a convention, all JavaScript code must be enclosed within *<script> </script>* tags, especially if you are writing the code within an HTML document. This is important so that the browser can tell the difference between JavaScript code and any other code used to build the website.

There are a lot of scripting languages available today. Bearing this in mind, always make sure you indicate the scripting language you use before you proceed as follows:

```
<script type ="text/javascript">
```

The following is an example of an HTML file with JavaScript:

```
<html>

<head>

        <title>JavaScript for Beginners</title>

        <script type="text/javascript">

                alert("Welcome to JavaScript");

        </script>

</head>

<body>

</body>
```

```
</html>
```

The convention above works well. If you are using HTML5, however, you do not necessarily need to write *type="text/javascript"*. The code will still work if it looks like the example below:

```
<html>

<head>

        <title>JavaScript for Beginners</title>

        <script>

                alert("Welcome to JavaScript");

        </script>

</head>

<body>

</body>

</html>
```

Variables in JavaScript

Variables are storage units for value and expressions. The general convention in most programming languages is that you must declare variables before you use them in a script. Variables are declared using the keyword *var* as shown below:

var name;

Values can be assigned to variables before or after you declare the variables as shown below:

var name = "Hannah";

or

var name;

name = "Hannah";

You are free to assign unique names to variables as you wish. However, it is always advisable that your variables have reasonable and meaningful names. Variables are case-sensitive and must always start with a letter. What this means is that the following variables, for example, are not the same:

total value

totalValue

Arrays

Arrays refer to objects that can hold a group of items. They come in handy when you are working with a very large set of data. All the data in the set must be similar. Assuming you are working with data for 100 pupils, you must create 100 variables in case you use variables. However, you can get the same results by using one array for all the pupils.

To pull data from an array, you call it with the index number assigned to it. Remember that in an array, the index of the first element is always zero. Here's an example:

var employees = ["Mary", "James", "Houston "];

In this array, the index of "Mary", "James", and "Houston" are 0, 1 and 2. To introduce more elements into this array, your code will be as follows:

pupils [3] = "Paula";

pupils [4] = "Sam";

Another option is to use an array constructor in the following manner:

var pupils = new Array("Mary", "James", "Houston");

Or

var pupils = new Array();

pupils[0] = "Mary";

pupils[1] = "James";

pupils[2] = "Houston";

There are several properties that define arrays, which enable programmers use them effectively. The following methods will help you find out the value or output of properties and methods used in arrays:

- push method – allows you to make values the last component in the array

- sort method – allows you to sort all the items in the array

- shift method – allows you to delete the first item in the array

- pop method – allows you to delete the last item in the array

- reverse method – allows you to change the order of items in the array

- prototype property – allows you to introduce new methods and properties to the array

- length property – allows you to determine the number of items in the array

Loops in JavaScript

The concept of loops is the same in all programming languages. Loops help you avoid writing the same code many times, reducing the risk of mistakes. When written properly loops will repeat a specific line or lines of code until a predefined condition is met.

Instead of writing the same line of code 50 or a thousand times, you can use only three or four lines with loops and get the same result.

Assuming you need to write the following code, it can be very cumbersome.

```
statement += ride[0] + "<br>";
statement += ride[1] + "<br>";
statement += ride[2] + "<br>";
statement += ride[3] + "<br>";
statement += ride[4] + "<br>";
statement += ride[5] + "<br>";
```

Alternatively, you can write a loop statement as follows:

```
var i;
for (i = 0; i < ride.length; i++) {
  statement += ride[i] + "<br>";
}
```

The types of loops used in JavaScript are discussed below:

- **for**

This loop repeats the code in a predetermined frequency. The syntax is as follows:

for (statement 1; statement 2; statement 3) {

write code

}

The syntax above means that statement 1 will be executed before the rest of the code. The second statement outlines the specific conditions which allow the execution of the code. The third statement will run each time the code block is executed.

Example:

```
for (i = 9; i < 15; i++) {
  text += "The number is " + i + "<br>";
}
```

In this example, the first statement means that the loop must only begin when the variable is 9 (var *i=9*).

The second statement outlines the condition necessary to run the loop. (i must be less than 15).

The third statement adds a value to *(i++)* every time the loop is executed.

While statement 1 is important, it is optional in JavaScript and the code will still work well without it. Statement 2 is also optional in JavaScript. If it holds true, the loop will repeat. However, if it is false, the loop terminates. In case you choose to do away with statement 2, remember to use a break within the loop. Without the break, the loop will continue indefinitely, probably crashing the browser.

- for/in

This loop repeats the code based on the specific properties outlined as shown below:

```javascript
var student = {fname:"Mary", lname:"Poppins", age:38};

var text = "";
var x;
for (x in student) {
  text += student[x];
}
```

- for/of

This loop repeats specific values of an object, like strings and arrays as shown below:

```javascript
var models = ['Toyota', 'Mercedes', 'Jaguar'];
var x;

for (x of models) {
```

```
document.write(x + "<br >");
}
```

- while

This loop repeats the code only if a given condition is true. The syntax is as follows:

```
while (condition) {

// write code

}
```

In the example below, this loop will persist as long as the variable in question *(i)* is less than 20:

```
while (i < 20) {
  text += "The result is " + i;
  i++;
}
```

- do/while

This loop repeats the code while a given condition is true. The syntax is as follows:

```
do {

// write code

}

while (condition);
```

Since the code is executed before the predefined condition is tested, the *do/while* loop will always run at least once. It runs whether the condition is true or not.

```
do {
  text += "The result is " + i;
  i++;
}
while (i < 20);
```

You will have realized by now that there is no difference between a *for* loop and a *while* loop, other than the omission of statements 1 and 3. Look at the examples below.

for loop to derive names of students from the students array:

```
var students = ["James", "Joan", "Sally", "Farid"];
var i = 0;
var text = "";

for (;students[i];) {
  text += students[i] + "<br>";
  i++;
}
```

while loop to derive names of students from the students array:

```
var students = ["James", "Joan", "Sally", "Farid"];
var i = 0;
var text = "";
```

```
while (students[i]) {
  text += students[i] + "<br>";
  i++;
}
```

Conditional Statements

The role of conditional statements is to determine how your code will run if certain conditions are met. JavaScript uses the following types of conditional statements:

- if

This statement executes a block of code if a specific condition is true as shown in the syntax below:

```
if (condition) {

//execute code if condition is true

}
```

Example:

Change the greeting to "Good evening" if the time is 7:00 p.m. or later.

```
if (hour > 19) {
```

greeting = "Good evening";

}

- **else**

This statement executes a block of code if a specific condition is false as shown in the syntax below:

if (condition) {

//execute code if condition is true

}

else {

//execute code if condition is false

}

Example:

Change the greeting to "Good evening" if the time is 7:00 p.m. or later. Otherwise, the greeting should read "Good day".

if (hour >19) {

greeting = "Good evening";

}

else {

greeting = "Good day";

}

- else/if

This statement specifies a condition to test if the first one returns false as shown in the syntax below:

if (condition1) {

//execute code if condition1 is true

}

else if (condition2) {

//execute code if condition1 is false but condition2 is true

}

else {

//execute code if condition1 and condition2 are false

Example:

Change the greeting to "Have a lovely morning" if time is it earlier than 9:00 a.m. Otherwise, if it is after 9:00 a.m., but before 7:00 p.m., change the greeting to

"Have a good day". Otherwise, change the greeting to "Have a lovely evening".

```
if (time < 9) {
  greeting = "Have a lovely morning";
} else if (time < 19) {
  greeting = "Have a good day ahead";
} else {
  greeting = "Have a lovely evening";
}
```

- **switch**

This statement executes alternative code from many blocks of code available as shown in the syntax below:

```
switch(statement) {
  case a:
    // execute code
    break;
  case b:
    // execute code
    break;
  default:
    // execute code
}
```

For example, the *getMonth* () code will return the months of the year between 0 and 11. (January =0, February=1, March=2...):

```
switch (new Date().getMonth()) {
  case 0:
```

```
      month = "January";
      break;
    case 1:
      month = "February";
      break;
    case 2:
       month = "March";
      break;
    case 3:
      month = "April";
      break;
    case 4:
      month = "May";
      break;
    case 5:
      month = "June";
      break;
    case 6:
      month = "July";
}
```

Functions in JavaScript

Functions are code blocks that are written with a specific role in mind. Functions are called in JavaScript, and the script executes them to perform the predefined role as shown below:

```
function myFunction (x1, x2) {
```

```
        return x1 * x2;

//function returns product of x1 and x2

}
```

Functions in JavaScript must be defined by the keyword *function*, their name, and enclosed in parentheses *()*. Function names follow the same rules prescribed for variables.

Assuming you have several lines of code that you will use frequently, it is wise to write a function that contains all the lines of code you need and call the function each time you need to use it, instead of writing the code again.

The code to be executed each time you call a function is written within the parenthesis. This is referred to as function invocation. Functions can be invoked automatically, when you click on a button or when the JavaScript code calls it.

Looped functions terminate when the JavaScript code finds a *return* statement. The return value is then displayed to the user as shown below:

```
var x = myFunction(2, 5);  // Call the function. Return
value              should           be           x

function myFunction(a,            b)              {
  return a * b;          // Function returns product
```

}

The result is 10

You have to be careful when using functions. Many times, people forget the operator *()*, yet this is what returns the function. Without the operator, you get the definition of the function instead of the result.

Cookies

Cookies are fragments of data your browser stores in your computer. They help to make your browsing experience faster and smoother, especially in retrieving data. One of the most popular cookies is that which allows you to save your login details so that you don't have to keep typing it into the browser all the time. They are stored in your computer as keys and their value pairs.

Cookies are helpful because they reduce the workload of your browser. Instead of contacting the server each time you make a request, the browser fetches the necessary information from the cookies.

The cookie's property is *document.cookie* as shown below:

document.cookie = "cookiename=cookievalue"

Depending on the kind of cookies you are using, you can add an expiry date so that your computer deletes the cookie after a specific time. Without an expiry date, the cookies are automatically deleted the moment you close your browser as shown below:

document.cookie = "cookiename=cookievalue; expires= Fri, 22 Aug, 2018 19:00:01 GMT "

Possible Challenges When Programming in JavaScript

JavaScript is one language that you interact with almost all the time you are online. Its applications are so numerous that you might not even realize when you are using it, beyond the browser. The fact that it is widely used makes it more susceptible to concerns, especially on the end-user's side.

JavaScript can be very frustrating, even when working with a very simple code. A very simple code error might interfere with everything else on your website. It gets worse when you have been coding for a very long time and are too tired to start looking for the error. The good thing is that most of the browsers today have been updated and can withstand some simple errors without interfering with the user's experience.

JavaScript often struggles with Bitwise functions. Conventionally, JavaScript will store numbers in 64-bit floating point format and operate them on a 32-bit format. To do this, it has to convert the integers back and forth. Constant conversion consumes a lot of time, and in the process, you spend more time running a script, interfering with the response. Systems that take a lot of time to render and are usually heavy on memory use too.

One of the flaws that JavaScript has is that it does not support multiple inheritance. There are a lot of programs that might need this feature, especially in object-oriented programming. Single inheritance alone is not sufficient for such programs.

A common concern among programmers is the lack of a debugging facility in JavaScript. There are a few HTML editors that can debug your code. However, this is not usually as efficient as you would expect in the editors used in C++ or even C. It gets even worse for you, because since you are unable to see the errors in your code, you might not detect them at all.

Every browser reads and interprets JavaScript in a unique way. Code that works perfectly on Microsoft Edge might not work well on Chrome or Safari. To manage this problem, you have to independently test your code on different browsers before you publish it. Once you do this for the current versions of the browsers, you also have to think about users who run older browsers. They also need the same support as the updated browser versions, so you must test and make sure your code renders properly on them too.

The end user can view the JavaScript code. This creates a security problem because a malicious user can use this to exploit your program. Since they have access to the source code, nothing stands in their way if they decide to use the code without seeking your authentication. Someone could easily use your hard work to make a lot of money without your knowledge, and without giving you the recognition you deserve. It is also possible that a hacker could intentionally add code into your website that will interfere with your security.

Another challenge you will experience when programming in JavaScript is that many times there are dynamic changes to the conventions that are sprung on users without any warning. Because JavaScript generally runs in an engine like Chakra on Microsoft Edge or Blink in Node and Chrome, it is not easy to stay informed.

In terms of access, the fact that someone can easily access your JavaScript from the browser means they can also disable it. If this happens, you will not render the website properly, the browser's memory consumption increases, and it might stop working altogether.

To understand how cumbersome the update process for JavaScript is, compare it with Python, for instance. While Python might be slow in some respects, the internal implementation and organization is relatively straightforward. You know what to expect and when, which is not the case with JavaScript.

Chapter 8:

Programming in Java

Java, not to be confused with JavaScript, is a programming language that has been around since 1995. It is one of the most popular languages today, especially when you consider the fact that billions of devices in use today are running Java. In particular, the prominent use of Java is evident in mobile applications, web applications, database connections, desktop applications, gaming, application and web servers, plus much more.

Given how many of these devices are in use and the prospect of advancement, Java is a language that will help you make strategic moves in as far as development and programming is concerned. There are several reasons why Java is an amazing language to learn, other than the fact that you have a better chance of getting contract offers in different development fields.

First of all, Java runs smoothly across a variety of operating systems. From Mac to Windows, Linux and even Raspberry Pi, Java will work just fine. Today people are more receptive to programs, languages and any other tech that is cross-platform, because it allows ease of use without necessarily having the users spend more on compatibility enhancements.

The popularity of Java is another reason why you would be best suited to learn the language. A popular language is one whose demand is incredible. This means in the development space, there will always be opportunities for programmers who can program in Java.

Another reason why you will find learning Java handy is the large community built around it. From users to developers, there is immense support, meaning that if you are ever writing code in Java and you run into problems, it is very easy to find a solution from experts all over the world. Chances are high that someone has had the same issue you have before or someone might have recently come up with a better way to solve your problem.

The world of computer programming today is focused on moving towards open-source development. Gone are the days when source codes would be a preserve of the few. Today people share code in programming communities online, improve on each other's code and learn from one another. Java is an open-source language. Therefore, you can look forward to free exchange of ideas, especially in terms of libraries and associated APIs.

Security is another issue that people usually worry about when programming in any language. With Java, you are not just guaranteed programming in a secure language, but at the same time you will also enjoy a powerful interface that runs efficiently without compromising on speed or consuming a lot of your computing resources.

Perhaps one of the best reasons why you should consider learning Java is that even without experience in programming, you can start learning Java, perfect your skills and go on to build amazing projects.

Java Syntax

Some computers come with Java pre-installed. If yours doesn't have it, you can download it online, install it and start writing code. Other than the Java SE Development Kit, you will only need your native text editor.

Each application in Java must always start with the class name, which has to be similar with the filename. For example, a Java file will look like this:

```
public class MyPeople                                    {
  public static void main(String[]        args)        {
    System.out.println("Meet        My        People");
                                                         }
}
```

The text file should be saved as *MyPeople.java*. To access this file, find it in your command prompt by typing in *"javac MyPeople.java"*.

If your code was written correctly and is free of errors, your system will compile it, prompting the next line without an error. In the next prompt, enter *"java MyPeople"* and the Java file will run.

The expected output should be:

Meet My People

All the code you write in Java must be within a class. In the example above, our class is *MyPeople*. Since Java is case-sensitive, classes must begin with a capital letter. This means that *MyPeople* and *mypeople* are not the same.

Another point you should always remember is that in Java, the class name and the file name must also match. You should also make sure all file names are saved with the *.java* extension.

All Java programs have a *main()*. Any code within this section is executed when you run the file.

Within the *main()* method, you will find the *println()* method that instructs the system to display the specified line of text on your screen.

As you have seen in other programming languages, your code must end in a semicolon in Java too.

Comments in Java

The role of a comment is to explain the code. This makes your work understandable. Comments will also keep you from executing the code during testing. There are single line and multiline comments.

Any content that follows the comment marks // is not executed when your code runs, as shown below:

// This comment will not print System.out.println("Meet My People");

Multiline comments must be closed. As above, any text within the /* and */ marks is not executed.

/* This comment will not print either */ System.out.println("Hello World");

Variables in Java

Variables store data values in each programming language. The following are the different types of variables you will use in Java:

- boolean – the values return true or false

- char – the values are enclosed in single quotes as follows 'g', or 'G'

- float – the values are for floating point numbers like 246.38

- int – these are whole number representatives like 246

- string – strings are text variables. They are enclosed in double quotes, for example "Welcome"

You must assign a value to variables before you call it. Variables are declared in the following manner:

type variable = value;

Here's an example:

```
String cars = "BMW";
System.out.println(cars);
```

The following example shows how to declare variables of the other data types used in Java:

```
int myNum = 9;
float myFloatNum = 4.21f;
char myLetter = 'E';
boolean myBool = false;
String myText = "Welcome";
```

Java is instructed to display the desired variables with the *println()* method. You can also combine variables and text using the + character as shown below:

```
String carName = "BMX ";
String carModel = "X1";
```

```
String carIdentity = carName + carModel;
System.out.println(carIdentity);
```

Output: *BMW X1.*

The example above can also be used with integers as shown below:

```
int a                                = 50;
int b                                = 10;
System.out.println(a + b); // Results value of a + b
```

The output should be *60.*

If you need to use many variables of the same type, you can use a comma to separate them as follows:

```
int a = 50, b = 10, c = 80;
System.out.println(a + b + c);
```

The unique names that are used to call variables in Java are called identifiers. You can use very short identifiers like a and b or descriptive terms like sum, height and length. When using identifiers, you cannot use Java keywords like *string, int* and *char.*

All identifiers must begin with a small letter and must never have a whitespace.

Data Types

There are five data types in Java: string, Boolean, character, floating point number and integer. These data types are further classified into two groups, primitive and non-primitive data types.

Primitive data types indicate the size of the value and the type of the values. Java uses the following primitive data types:

- **boolean (1 bit)**

Store data whose value will return either true or false, as shown below:

```
boolean isSheHungry                     = false;
boolean areYouHappy                     = true;
System.out.println(isSheHungry);   // Returns false
System.out.println(areYouHappy);   // Returns true
```

- **byte (1 byte)**

Stores whole numbers between -128 and 127. You can use *byte* instead of *int* as shown below:

```
byte myNum = 89;

System.out.println (myNum);
```

- **char (2 bytes)**

Store single character values as shown below:

```
char carRating                          = 'A';
System.out.println(carRating);
```

- **double (8 bytes)**

Stores fractional numbers between 1.7e-308 and 1.7e+308. The values must end in *d* as shown below:

double myNum = 32.35d;
System.out.println(myNum);

- **float (4 bytes)**

Stores numbers with decimal points. The value must always end with an *f* as shown below:

float myNum = 92.26f;
System.out.println(myNum);

- **int (4 bytes)**

Stores whole numbers between -2147483648 and 2147483647 as shown below:

int myNum = 3613;
System.out.println(myNum);

- **long (8 bytes)**

Stores whole numbers between -9223372036854775808 and 9223372036854775807. Remember that all the values must end in *L* as shown below:

long myNum = 22745194639L;
System.out.println(myNum);

This type of data is used when you need more space than available in *int*.

- short (2 bytes)

Stores whole numbers between -32768 and 32767 as shown below:

short myNum = 6670;
System.out.println(myNum);

Further to the information above, primitive data types are classified into integer types (storing negative and positive whole numbers) and floating-point types (storing fractional numbers).

Non-primitive data types

This type of data refers to specific items, so they are also known as reference data types. Other than *string*, non-primitive data types are not predefined in Java as is the case with primitive data types. You define the type of data according to your present needs.

You can use non-primitive data types to call methods and perform tasks that you would not manage to do with primitive data types. You will also realize that while all the primitive data types always have a value, non-primitive data types do not necessarily need to. Therefore, you can have their value as *null* where applicable.

In contrast with the primitive data types, non-primitive data types must begin with a capital letter. More importantly, they all have the same size while the sizes of primitive data types are varied.

Type Casting in Java

Type casting refers to a situation where you assign one primitive data type the value of another. You can either narrow cast or widen cast.

Widening casting is an automatic process where a small data size is passed into a larger data size as shown below:

```
public class StudentWeight {
  public static void main(String[] args) {
    int myInt = 52;
    double myDouble = myInt; // Cast: int to double

    System.out.println(myInt);     // Outputs 52
    System.out.println(myDouble);   // Outputs 52.88
  }
}
```

On the other hand, narrow casting is a manual process. Make sure you enclose the type in a parenthesis before the value affected as shown below:

```
public class Studentweight {
  public static void main(String[] args) {
    double myDouble = 52.88;
    int myInt = (int) myDouble; // Manual cast: double
to int

    System.out.println(myDouble);   // Outputs 52.88
    System.out.println(myInt);      // Outputs 52
  }
}
```

Math Computation in Java

There are lots of mathematical operations that you can perform in Java as shown in the following examples:

- To determine the highest value between a and b - *Math.max(a,b)*

Math.max (25,37)

- To determine the lowest value between a and b – *Math.min(a,b)*

Math.min (25,37)

- To determine the square root of a – *Math.sqrt(a)*

Math.sqrt(81)

Booleans in Java

Booleans are very specific in the values they return. The result is either true or false, on or off, yes or no. You can also use comparison operators to deliver a Boolean value from a Boolean expression as shown below:

```
int a = 201;
int b = 76;
System.out.println(a > b); // returns true, because 201
is higher than 76
```

```
int a = 201;

System.out.println(201 == 76); // returns false,
because 201 is not equal to 76
```

```
int a = 201;
System.out.println(a == 201); // returns true, because
the value of a is equal to 201
```

Conditional Statements

The following logical conditions are used in Java:

- Equal to *(==)*

- Not equal to *(!=)*

- Greater than *(>)*

- Greater than or equal to *(>=)*

- Less than *(<)*

- Less than or equal to *(<=)*

In as far as conditional statements are concerned, the following conditional statements are used in Java:

- If – executes a block of code if given condition is true.

```
if (condition) {
 // execute code
}
```

The following example returns a comparison between two integers:

```
if (132 > 74) {
  System.out.println("132 is greater than 74");
}
```

- Else – executes a block of code if given condition is false.

```
if (condition) {
 // execute code
} else {
```

```
//execute code

}
```

The following example returns a student's performance in an exam:

```
int grade = 78;
if (grade < 64) {
  System.out.println("Pass.");
} else {
  System.out.println("Fail.");
}
// Outputs "Fail."
```

- Else/if – test a new condition if the first one is false.

```
if (condition1) {
  // execute code if condition1 is true
} else if (condition2) {
  // execute code if condition1 is false and condition2
is true
} else {
  // execute code if condition1 and condition2 is false
}
```

The following example returns a student's performance in an exam:

```
int grade = 88;
if (grade < 64) {
  System.out.println("Pass.");
```

```
} else if (grade < 78) {
 System.out.println("Average");
} else {
 System.out.println("Fail.");
}
// Outputs "Fail."
```

- Switch – executes alternative code to execute from several.

```
switch(expression) {
 condition a:
  // execute code
  break;
 condition b:
  // execute code
  break;
 default:
  // execute code
}
```

The following is an example of a switch code to return the results of a team's games:

```
int game = 3;
switch (game) {
 condition 1:
  System.out.println("Win");
  break;
 condition 2:
  System.out.println("Draw");
  break;
 condition 3:
```

```java
    System.out.println("Loss");
    break;
  condition 4:
    System.out.println("Void");
    break;
  condition 5:
    System.out.println("Postponed");
    break;
  condition 6:
    System.out.println("Canceled");
    break;
  condition 7:
    System.out.println("Abandoned");
    break;
}
// Outputs "Loss" (Condition 3)
```

Possible Challenges When Programming in Java

Java is widely used in programming. With billions of devices running on Java each day, it is difficult to imagine that this language might have some serious challenges too. However, there are always two sides to every coin. As you learn to program in Java, the following are some of the issues that you might realize.

Practically, Java is one of the slowest programming languages you will come across. You might not realize this as a beginner because you are probably still learning the ropes and getting excited with all the new information. The possibilities that lie ahead of you might cloud this judgement. However, once you have tried working with different languages, you will come to realize how slow Java is.

There are several reasons why Java might be as slow as it is. The problem could be your bandwidth or perhaps your compiler is not properly optimized. These are things you can change. However, even if you do that, the byte-code interpretation for Java programs is generally sluggish. Java is so slow that C++ seems extremely faster. Some experts believe C++ is more than 30 times faster than Java.

Many hacks have in the recent past been executed by exploiting loopholes in Java code. This is something that you cannot afford to risk today. Many developers and programmers have since had to reconsider using Java as a result of this. Given that it is one of the most popular and widely used languages in devices all over the world, the prospects of a successful hack are very serious.

Most recently, Oracle decided to charge commercial license to programmers for using Java. This is quite a bummer, given that many programmers and developers are increasingly moving towards open-source programming.

It gets worse, the caveat that Oracle imposed over the use of Java is that you need a commercial license to access patches, updates and bug fixes for each user or processor. You can still use the free version of Java, but there will be limitations from time to time.

Java does struggle with performance from time to time. Given that it is a high-level language, this does not come as a surprise. The reason for this is because it has to operate with the efficiency of a virtual machine, which is quite a stretch. Some features, like garbage collector, can consume more than 25% of your CPU when in use. This is a feature that you cannot do without but will impede the performance of your computer. As a result, you must invest in very powerful devices to run Java smoothly.

Java code can be very complex. A lot of languages today try to make their syntax easy to understand by making them as close to normal language as possible. However, the problem with this is that it creates too much commotion in the code, and that might render the code difficult to scan or read.

When programming in Java, you will struggle to create a GUI that is appealing to the end user. In fact, many programmers have to use other tools to get around this. You will need additional tools, especially when creating programs that must maintain their native feel when deployed. This is something you will not find in Java.

If you have limited time to work on a project, Java is not one of the best options you should consider. The reason for this is because it uses latency critical tuning and the options available are very limited. You are better off coding in a different language altogether to spare time.

Garbage collection in Java is not controlled. This is a problem because as a programmer, you need express privilege over garbage collection. Simple code functions like *free()* and *delete()* are not provided in Java.

Chapter 9:

Raspberry Pi - An

Overview

Raspberry Pi is an assembled printed circuit board. It does not have an operating system or even a power supply. It is a micro Linux machine the size of a credit card.

The concept behind Raspberry Pi was to build a machine that could enable developers and users to enhance their programming skills, and at the same time accord students a good learning environment with which they can improve their understanding of different hardware they come across.

Raspberry Pi is one of the best-selling computer models in the world at the moment, given that it is a very small computer that can be plugged into your display. When you purchase Raspberry Pi, what you are buying is essentially the board. The SD card and power supply are bought separately.

By design, other than the primary chip, Raspberry Pi is open hardware. The primary chip controls the memory, graphics, CPU and USB controller among other functional essentials.

There are different Raspberry Pi models in the market, with the most recent being Raspberry Pi 3. All the models released so far run on the Raspbian RaspBMC operating system, use HDMI composite RCA video output and are powered through the Micro USB slot.

There are lots of things that you can do with a Raspberry Pi. It is one device that is suitable for creatives, given the impressive projects that you can build with it. Some of the notable projects that have been built with Raspberry Pi include a dicta-teacher, that was designed to help blind children learn how to read braille, working as a web or media server and the impressive high altitude balloons that the North Carolina Near Space Research used to take amazing photos of the earth from space.

What this shows us is how much potential there is when using Raspberry Pi. One of the perks of using Raspberry Pi is that it is a very affordable device. For around $35, you can own the Raspberry Pi and begin your foray into creative development.

Raspberry Pi 3 – Software Specifications

Raspberry Pi security patches and updates are released frequently. It is wise to keep your device updated, especially to patch bugs in its design. You can update the Raspberry Pi through a terminal command as follows:

sudo apt update

This code updates the internal software database for your Raspberry Pi. In so doing, your Raspberry Pi will be able to determine the best and current updates when they are available.

You can also run the following code:

sudo apt dist-upgrade

This code downloads all the available updates and installs all of them.

There is also the option of *rpi-update*. To be on the safe side, never run this code unless you are expressly advised by an expert. The reason for this is because this specific code updates the Raspberry Pi firmware and your Linux kernel to the most recent version available. While this is a good thing, the most recent version might be in beta testing stage, which could render your Raspberry Pi unstable.

Raspberry Pi 3 – Model B Hardware Specifications

- 1200 – 1400 MHz

- 512MB – 1GB RAM

- 1-4 USB ports

- 1000 Base ethernet connectivity

- 2.5A power supply

Depending on the Raspberry Pi model you purchase, your device will come with either 26 or 40 interface pins.

Configuring Raspberry Pi

The following steps will help you boot and set up your Raspberry Pi:

- Insert the memory card into your Raspberry Pi

- Connect the keyboard via USB

- Connect your HDMI cable

- Check to make sure your internet is properly set-up

- Plug in the USB power supply

Once everything is ready, sign into your Raspberry Pi. The default settings should be username: *pi* and password *raspberry*.

Raspberry Pi 3 comes with in-built wireless settings, so it will scan for available networks by keying in the following:

pi@raspberrypi: ~ $ sudo iwlist wlan0 scan

Add the wpa supplicant file for your wireless network as follows:

pi@raspberrypi:~ $ sudo nano /etc/wpa_supplicant/wpa_supplicant.conf

This prompt brings up the Nano editor through which you can input the wireless network details as follows:

```
network={
 ssid="yourwifiName"
 psk="yourwifiPassword"
}
```

Enter the network details then press *Ctrl+x* to save the details. You will get a prompt to confirm the details, press *Y* and then *Enter*.

Reboot your device to ensure the settings are correctly configured and stored:

pi@raspberrypi: ~ $ sudo reboot

Upon reboot:

pi@raspberrypi: ~ $ ipcongif wlan0

If you entered the correct details, this prompt should give you the IP address in the following syntax:

inet addr: 192.168.1.1

Remember to write the address down somewhere because you will need it to connect to other devices where necessary.

Programming in Raspberry Pi

One of the core ideas behind Raspberry Pi was to enable students to grasp programming at an early age. The Pi in Raspberry Pi actually alludes to Python programming.

Since the introduction of Raspberry Pi, many programming languages have been ported into the device. This is either by the language developers or users who simply needed to have a shot at their favorite language on such an amazing device. The good thing about this is that there is a very wide resource base for anyone who needs help with any language that can be ported onto Raspberry Pi.

The following programming languages can be used in Raspberry Pi:

- **Python**

In programming, one of the reasons why Python is popular is its syntax. It is easy to learn, and programmers can do so much work without writing many code blocks as they used to in C and other languages. Code that can be written in two to four lines in Python could possibly take at least eight lines in C.

- **Erlang**

This programming language is used in instances where developers need to eliminate the possibility of failure. These are usually high-profile environments, like traffic control systems or developers in nuclear power plants. Programs written in Erlang are critical, as failure in their missions would likely be disastrous and have far-reaching effects.

The concept of Erlang is such that several computers run specific programs concurrently. Each of the computers can pick up and keep the system running in case one of them is inaccessible. Therefore, for such critical situations, the system must never go offline.

- **Scratch**

This is one of the basic programming languages available with the Raspberry Pi. The idea behind Scratch is to enable young people learn how to solve simple computational and math problems through programming, while at the same time having fun.

- C

C is a programming language upon which most of the languages we know today are built. There are lots of systems currently that run on C, including operating systems. In fact, the Linux operating system that powers Raspberry Pi is mostly written in C.

- C++

This general-purpose language was built to improve on C, which is basically the foundation of programming. There are so many devices and systems that are running C++, including games, applications and embedded programs in mobile devices.

- Java

One of the perks of learning to code in Java is that it bridged the gap between developers, programming languages and user systems. Programs written in Java could be used on any device, without forcing the developer to rewrite their code. Through Java, developers could simply write code in the language they are familiar with and it would be compiled on any device without a hitch.

- JavaScript

JavaScript allows you to interact with your web browsers effectively. It works alongside HTML and

CSS to enhance user experiences. In as far as client-side scripting is concerned, JavaScript makes work easier for users and developers alike.

- HTML5

This is the foundation of the internet. HTML informs the browser of the structure of the website and how different pages are linked together. HTML5 is an innovative redesign of HTML, which allows developers to create apps and websites that can run effectively on tablets, smartphones and any other portable device that users have access to.

- Perl

Perl is one of the most adaptable and flexible programming languages so far. It is the programming language responsible for the dynamic websites and content that we access online. Many popular websites that we access daily have the amazing user interfaces we enjoy because of Perl, such as eBay and Amazon.

- jQuery

This is a JavaScript library, probably one of the most widely used. jQuery runs on web browsers, allowing them to script HTML files efficiently. Through jQuery, developers can easily create interactive content and interfaces online with limited knowledge of JavaScript.

Accessories for Your Raspberry Pi 3 – Model B

Looking at the languages that you can program in Raspberry Pi, it is evident that this is one device that will change the world. These languages cover a wide spectrum, narrowing down on virtually everything we use online. There are a lot of accessories that you can use with the Raspberry Pi. Here are some of the popular ones you can come across:

- Infrared camera

- Camera

- Gertboard

- Hardware Attached on Top (HAT)

- Temperature sensor

- LCD touchscreens

Sample Project Ideas for Your Raspberry Pi

The following are some of the projects that you can build through your Raspberry Pi:

- **Web hosting**

It is possible to host websites on your Raspberry Pi, especially if you are running a WordPress website. Some of the skills that you will learn include PHP, MySQL and Apache, all which come in handy when hosting and managing websites. Other than that, you can actually build a fully functional website off WordPress on your Raspberry Pi, host and update content on it frequently.

- **Server services**

There are different types of server services that you can run on Raspberry Pi. from Apache servers to VPN servers, Raspberry Pi accords you the chance to create an affordable server, reducing your current spending in case you are using some of the popular options available.

- **Build a laptop**

Raspberry Pi is in itself a computer. In fact, one of the concepts behind Raspberry Pi is to help users understand how computers work. With in-depth knowledge of Raspberry Pi, you can simply build your own laptop from scratch, complete with a keyboard, trackpad and screen.

- **Penetration testing**

If you are a penetration tester, one of the best things you can access at the moment is Raspberry Pi. It is a portable device, which allows you to target specific networks and learn more about them. Once you install Kali, a Linux distro specially designed for hacking, you can conduct tests on networks.

Risks and Benefits of Using Raspberry Pi

Given that Raspberry Pi is a very affordable single board computer, it is wise to give it a shot, especially since it is primarily designed to encourage learning and education. It is possible to install a fully operational OS on Raspberry Pi.

Considering the cost, this will probably be one of the most affordable computers you can ever own. It gets even better because you can build it from scratch and affix the hardware specifications you desire.

Raspberry Pi is easily the best link to the Internet of Things and associated devices. This is possible through the General Purpose Input Output pins (GPIO). Conventional computers do not have this feature. Through Raspberry Pi, therefore, you can easily connect the pins to external components and sensors, allowing you the ability to program in unique languages you understand and interact with many new-age devices that are being built under the IoT.

While the older models of the Raspberry Pi did not have wireless capacity and you had to use ethernet connection, current models have been improved. You can now enjoy wireless and Bluetooth connectivity, allowing you to build projects on Raspberry Pi remotely.

While these benefits are encouraging, there are risks involved in using Raspberry Pi too. First, the Raspberry Pi does not come with fuse protection like normal computers do. Therefore, it is up to you to determine the right power limit. This increases the risk of damaging your chipboard if you do not connect the pins properly.

For a computer that you can get for around $35, surely you cannot expect it to perform at the peak speeds that you get from machines that cost thousands of dollars. Its memory is limited, and while it can perform a variety of tasks comfortably, it would be a stretch if you pushed the limits.

Conclusion

Raspberry Pi might be a lot of awesome things, but it is not a beast of a device. This prevents it from probably serving at the same potential that you would expect of a computer. The memory capacity is limited, and since you cannot expand it as you would with a desktop PC or your laptop, your utility is also limited.

The best way to get into the world of programming is to learn the basics. The languages introduced in this book are not just the basics of computer programming, but they are the most important languages you will ever learn. Everything you do in programming from now on will be a variation of these languages, unless of course you create a new language, which requires some level of genius.

Computers are all around us, meaning that programming is all around you too. There is so much you can learn and a lot more that you can do with the knowledge you gain from this book. The idea of a programming bible is to help you have a reference point whenever you need to refresh your memory about something, as you might need to check a few things from time to time. Many times, it is the simple things that we take for granted that eventually make a big difference.

All the languages you have learned in this book will help you set foot in the world of programming better than anyone else might. This book covers the key languages that you will use whether in developing apps, websites, games or even if you are just an enthusiast who cannot keep away from writing code.

Once you dive into programming, everything else becomes a walk in the park. You can choose how to grow your career in programming, or you can decide to combine programming with something else, like networking. Whichever direction your career goes, rest assured that you will always have something to fall back on when things are tough.

The world of tech is constantly evolving. Some changes happen as fast as a few months, others last a while. You must keep learning and reminding yourself of the key concepts so that when changes take place in your niche you know how to respond to them, as well as how to prepare yourself for the advancements that come with the changes.

In any development environment, you might realize that many organizations tend to slack when it comes to installing updates or upgrading their languages. Do not be in a hurry to upgrade to the latest version. More often, the earliest version of an update is buggy.

When an update is rolled out, you can try the new version on a test machine that is isolated from your main machine. These tests can help you understand the new changes, the impact that they have, and more importantly, test to see if they have an adverse effect on your code. Without testing, you can run the upgrade and mess up with work that has taken you months or years to accomplish. It is better to be safe than sorry, especially when it comes to upgrades.

While there are a lot of programming languages, including many others which have not been covered in this book, the ones mentioned here will shape your future and the future of the world. You can try mastering as many of them as you can. This will make you a versatile programmer, capable of handling different project specifications and capable of taking on a new challenge. A dynamic world requires dynamic thinkers to tackle the impossible. If you believe this describes you, learn as much as you can.

At the same time, you must also be aware of your limitations when it comes to programming. There is no point in trying to learn the whole world and mastering nothing. This could easily lead to fatigue and you might also lose enthusiasm about programming. Do not just read the languages, research on the kind of projects that you can build with them. This might also give you an idea of what to focus your practice and lessons on.

Programming is usually a resource intensive field. This does not just involve the memory and other computing specifications; it is also about you. Personally, you have a lot to invest in programming if you are to succeed. Your time will be worth a lot more in programming when you master a specific language that suits your career path. If you can do that, every moment you spend coding will eventually pay off.

Granted, you will end up spending a lot of time writing code. However, you must also take care of yourself. It would be pointless to become one of the best programmers when you cannot enjoy the fruits of your labor because of deteriorating health. This is something that many programmers struggle with and you might too.

Learn to take a break. The world will not crash and burn when you step away from the keyboard. Give yourself enough room to think, brainstorm, do something else that gets your mind away from programming. In the long run, it will pay off.

Programming will require that you are always working on a network or connected to one. Beyond programming, you must learn to disconnect. Spare time and step away from the computer. Talk to people and engage in activities outdoors. You should not run the risk of losing your humanity in writing code. Code can and will always be improved upon.

Someone will write better code tomorrow than what you wrote today, and life goes on. However, the connections and moments you miss in life will never come back. You can be a well-rounded programmer, living a complete and happy life without giving up programming.

Whether you are starting as a beginner or if you have been in the industry for a while, there is never an end to learning. As mentioned earlier in the book, programming is like math. You have to keep practicing to be good at it. Computer languages like Python might be so close to the language you use to communicate with people around you, but they are not the same thing. You must allow yourself sufficient practice to get used to these languages. Familiarize with the keywords, variables, strings, functions, conditional statements and anything else that sets different languages apart from one another.

You are not alone in programming. Whether you are a beginner or not, there are millions, if not billions, of other programmers out there that you can learn from. Find useful resource centers, discussion groups and forums online. Go to Reddit, GitHub and any other platform where you can interact with other programmers. This will be one of the best learning experiences ever.

You will not just learn more about programming and different languages, you will also learn about some of the amazing things people are doing with programming out there. You will learn about new updates before they are rolled out, possible risks so you can mitigate and protect your device from hackers and so many other benefits. Better yet, you might even get a chance to collaborate with some of the best programmers in the world and become part of a team that builds one of the most amazing inventions of your time.

With programming, anything is possible.

References

Computer Programming - Quick Guide. (n.d.). Retrieved from **https://www.tutorialspoint.com/computer_progra mming/computer_programming_quick_guide.ht m**

What are Computer Programming Languages? (n.d.). Retrieved from **https://www.computerscience.org/resources/com puter-programming-languages/**